RADICAL OBEDIENCE

RADICAL
OBEDIENCE.

THE ETHICS OF RUDOLF BULTMANN

by

Thomas C. Oden

with a Response by Rudolf Bultmann

THE WESTMINSTER PRESS

PHILADELPHIA

PUBLISHED BY THE WESTMINSTER PRESS®
PHILADELPHIA, PENNSYLVANIA 19107
PRINTED IN THE UNITED STATES OF AMERICA

To THREE TEACHERS:

Albert C. Outler, who has awakened many
to the vitality of the historic
Christian tradition;

H. Richard Niebuhr, who taught us the
difference between God and the gods;

Joseph W. Mathews, in whose life has
been manifest radical obedience to
the divine demand.

Omnis recta cognitio
ab obedientia nascitur.
—Calvin

CONTENTS

PREFACE

WHAT IS THE MEANING of obedience to God? This is not a novel question for the historical Christian community, but its return to centrality in recent theological reflection may perplex modern men who have consigned this issue to a premodern era. For the question itself is associated with orthodoxy, reaction, self-righteousness, archaism, pietism, and fanaticism.

Increasingly as we become awakened to the current theological discussion on obedience, however, we are forced to give up many of our preconceptions about the question itself. For the theologians who are raising this question today speak of obedience to God as an onslaught against our self-righteousness. If their ethics are reactionary, then their mode of reaction is a jarringly revolutionary attack on all legalism and moralism. If this dialogue is fanaticism, it is taking place in the erudite context of historical and contemporary academic inquiry. If this conversation is either pious or orthodox, it is at least self-consciously critical of the traditions of both pietism and orthodoxy.

It is a disappointing feature of the English language that the word "obedience" does not convey the full dimension of "response" that is significantly present in

9

Hebrew, Greek, and German terms. Hebrew psychology tended to regard hearing as a complex operation involving the whole attention and total response of the hearer, and yet as a single process moving from hearing to approval or disapproval, and immediately on to obedience or disobedience.[1] The Hebrew did not dissect or separate the phenomena of hearing, willing, and acting. Hebrew has no special word for "obey." It simply has the word "hear" (*shema*) and its associates. The greek *hupakouō*, the Latin *oboedire*, and the German *Gehorsam* all follow the Hebrew pattern in expressing obedience as a *hearing-answering response*.[2] Unfortunately the present usage of the English "obedience" has dropped almost entirely the connotation of *response* to a heard word and merely conveys the impoverished notion of subordination to a higher authority.

If the dimension of hearing and responding belongs inseparably to the Biblical understanding of obedience, then any contemporary discussion of Christian obedience must be essentially an inquiry into the nature of *responsibility* before God and of *hearing* and answering God's address. If we keep constantly in mind that our English language does not freight the full meaning of the Biblical understanding of responsibility in the term "obedience," we can better perceive the deeper intention of the German discussion of *Gehorsam*.

I am particularly indebted in this endeavor to the late Dr. H. Richard Niebuhr, who not only presented me with a standard of excellence in his own teaching and writing that has been a wellspring from which I have constantly benefited, but also gave me wise and penetrating counsel throughout my graduate studies. Since this study was originally a part of a dissertation presented for the degree of doctor of philosophy at Yale University in 1960 under the title "The Idea of Obedience in Contemporary Protestant Ethics," I would like to express special thanks to the theological faculty of Yale University. Likewise for the interest that Dr. Bultmann has shown in my attempt critically to analyze his ethics, I feel most grateful.

I wish to express a special word of thanks to my former colleague, Schubert M. Ogden, upon whom I have depended many times for special assistance in translation and interpretation. Although I have sincerely differed with him, it has always been with great admiration for his brilliance, theological honesty, and erudite knowledge of the sources. If the following pages contain some criticisms of his burgeoning theological efforts, they are presented with sincere gratitude for the many hours spent in dialogue as neighbors. It is also in more than a perfunctory sense that I acknowledge the helpful counsel of Dr. David Shipley, who greatly assisted me in structuring the original inquiry, and Prof. Edward Hobbs, who first fired my interest in Bultmann studies. A grant by the National Council on Religion in Higher Education of a Kent Fellowship provided assistance for this study which has been deeply appreciated. Also I am especially grateful for dialogical encounter with three of my former colleagues at Perkins School of Theology, John W. Deschner, Van Harvey, and Robert Elliott, and subsequently my colleague at Phillips Seminary, Eugene Peters, whose constant stimulus and candid criticism have kept this project in a continual state of reappraisal. For stylistic criticism of the manuscript I am most grateful for the services of Decherd H. Turner, librarian at Perkins School of Theology, and Kay Scott. I would also wish to mention the names of Dr. Ulrich Mauser, Dr. James M. Robinson,

E. A. Pokorny, and W. T. Oden, to each of whom I am grateful for some particular help without which this project would not have been completed in good order. Finally, there is one person who has shared in this undertaking from start to finish and for whose help no acknowledgment can do justice: my wife, Edrita.

T. C. O.

Phillips Seminary
Enid, Oklahoma

INTRODUCTION

The Malaise of Current Protestant Ethics

THE EXCITING DAYS of the Niebuhrs and Tillich seem to be passing, leaving us with many persistent frustrations, and perhaps more demoralized than ever before. Having emerged from the creative ferment of the thirties and forties, the postliberal theologians and frontiersmen in ethics have achieved many of their aims. That period of intense productivity has hardly been matched by any achievement of the fifties, and it can be persuasively argued that its creative thrust has entirely spent itself. There are signs that indicate that we are experiencing an era of Protestant ethics characterized by moral paralysis, confusion, and demoralization more than decisiveness, vitality, and clear self-identity.

We who are of the second generation of this heritage of theological renewal must ask ourselves: How is this tradition to be carried forward with new vitality without becoming enmeshed in the nihilism that characterizes our time? How may we better perceive and understand the inadequacies of our fathers' generation while improving and elaborating their achievements? Can we diagnose the sick elements of our recent history before they become chronic?

Three features of our present condition deserve special

attention: (1) the pervasive sense of moral ambiguity, (2) the divorce of ethics and exegesis, and (3) the hiatus between a high Christology and actual Christian obedience. These three perplexities, although widely shared among Protestant ethicists, may be closely linked with the inadequacies and unfulfilled expectations of the efforts of three determinative leaders in Protestant theology: Reinhold Niebuhr, Paul Tillich, and Dietrich Bonhoeffer. Although none could circumspectly deny that each of these figures has made Promethean contributions to contemporary Protestant thought, the overall result of their work in ethics can only be assessed as a somewhat mixed blessing, inasmuch as some of the most recalcitrant current problems have in certain ways been aggravated by their work. If each has bequeathed a rich store to Protestantism, then it must also be said that certain refinements, corrections, and improvements need to be made in the pattern and tempo that they have undoubtedly set for Protestant ethics in our time.

Our purpose now shall be to scrutinize each of these perplexities with a view toward asking how the ethical proposals of Rudolf Bultmann may hold some promise of a fresh beginning point in each of these three phases of the malaise of current Protestant ethics.

1. A principal symptom of our predicament about which we must be more self-critical is *the prevailing sense of moral ambiguity* in Protestant ethics. We have learned our lesson all too well, especially from Reinhold Niebuhr *et al.*, that our finite, historical moral situation is essentially and persistently ambiguous. Consequently we have been tempted to a radical cynicism about all aggressive, decisive moral action.[1]

The extreme activism that has typified an earlier American religious consciousness has grown progressively senile since Niebuhr's *Moral Man and Immoral Society* (1932),[2] partly to our comfort and partly to our shame. That American Protestant social ethics is today "languishing in the tepid atmosphere of impotent confusion, passive bewilderment, and a pervasive sense of moral ambiguity"[3] can hardly be denied by a perceptive observer.

If there ever was a day when American Protestantism needed to be told that its social programs and causes should not be identified with the will of God, and that all moral action is ambiguous, such is not the need of our day, where the stifling air of an imperative-less ethics has caused all our moral striving to be paralyzed, or at least a bit tubercular.[4]

The deepest hunches of our times may have been sounded by the beatnik and nihilist, although in a conformist society they would hardly be counted as representative. License to do nothing in the midst of ponderous moral ambiguities has become the spurious moral privilege of the new Protestant ethic. We increasingly rationalize our response to the world of need with a sense of indifference which can hardly be called authentic Christian freedom. An ethic of grace has been construed as an ethic of license, indifference, and quiet brooding over the ambiguities of life.

American Protestant ethics has well learned the bitter truth that it can no longer honestly base its moral decisions on a perfectionist self-image. Robbed of our most reliable basis for moral action, self-righteousness, we now find ourselves caught in the unexpected situation of being incapable of decision and action, since we can no longer understand ourselves under our old perfectionist self-image. The driving sense of moral imperative that characterized earlier periods of American Protestantism has

vanished. Today it is tragically difficult for us to commit
ourselves to any moral action, since we have learned our
lesson all too well that, on the one hand, many legitimate
claims are in conflict in any given decision, and, on the
other hand, any alternative is sinful, since it involves our
calculation to protect our own interests.[5]

To be sure, American Protestants still have strong
moral emotions, feeling indignation and strong moral
righteousness for our own causes, but these emotions are
often merely a mask behind which lies a hollow sense of
moral ambiguity. The greatest temptation of American
Protestant ethics today is not a pride, which would identify its cause with God's will, but a moral insensitivity and
dullness that remains unresponsive to the imperative chal-
lenge of the contemporary human tragedy. We may be
justly disturbed and conscience-stricken that contemporary theology and ethics are not providing American
Protestantism with an authentic basis for conscientious
moral action, grounded not in the self-righteousness of
perfectionist moralism, but upon the distinctive claim of
the Christian gospel to love our neighbor as God has loved
us. Let us be ashamed, and let us be guilty that much
contemporary theology confronts us with only the most
feeble and innocuous moral *requirements,* sometimes even
unconsciously condoning an irresponsible cynicism toward all human striving. Liberal sentimentalism has faded
and been replaced by a neosentimentalism that would
offer us gospel without law, God's love without a demand
for an appropriate human response, freedom without
obedience, and an inconsequential indicative without an
imperative.

The heart of our dilemma is that the new theology has
justly undercut the inauthentic basis for moral action in

humanistic liberalism without supplying a new basis for constructive moral action and consequently left American Protestantism with a fragmented, stunted, and incapacitated sense of requirement and obligation to the neighbor and to society.[6] If the only basis for a genuine sense of moral imperative is self-righteousness, then there can be no Christian moral imperative. But the Christian kerygma provides a basis for strenuous moral action other than self-righteousness, viz., gratitude for the gifts of God in creation and redemption.

The answer to our dilemma lies in three directions: (1) the rediscovery of the classic Protestant understanding of the relation of gospel and law; (2) making relevant the message of the forgiveness of God to the man who knows that his situation is morally ambiguous, enabling him to act precisely *amid* conflicting claims, not regarding himself as righteous, but acting in the knowledge that he is forgiven even while he is choosing wrongly; (3) the recovery of some notion of the clarity of the demand of God, and reassessment of some of our hasty generalizations that the demand of God is ambiguous.

Rudolf Bultmann has been anticipating our needs in all three of these directions. Although we will allow full explication of his position subsequently to appear, we can now indicate that Bultmann's efforts in ethics have vigorously affirmed the interrelation of gospel and law,[7] and tried to reframe the message of forgiveness in demythologized language that contemporary man can appropriate. The notion of the *Einsichtigkeit* (discernibility) of the demand of God is one of the cornerstones of Bultmann's view of radical obedience.

The assertion that the demand of God is clear should not be viewed as wholly inconsistent with the efforts of

such persons as Reinhold Niebuhr to point to the ambiguity of concrete moral situations in which self-assertive
men participate.[8] We must learn to affirm the complexity
of the moral situation of estranged man without denying
the simplicity of the Word of God. We must learn to
weigh the Niebuhrian "nicely calculated less and more"
of discriminating moral decisions without failing to listen
for the situational clarity of the claim of God. We must
learn to affirm the contextual ambiguity of fallen man's
perception of the clear Word of God without denying the
Word which has chosen and chooses to make itself clear
amid our ambiguous history.

2. A second symptom of the malaise of current Protestant ethics is the stubborn and inflexible *divorce between
ethics and exegesis*.[9] If both Ernst Käsemann and Hermann Diem[10] have urgently called for a clarification of the
relation of exegesis and dogmatics, we are suggesting that
a similar *rapprochement* is due with respect to the relation between exegesis and ethics.

In its desire to achieve autonomous status, Protestant
social ethics has tended increasingly to dismiss and ignore
its Reformation heritage of *sola scriptura* and instead to
consider ethics increasingly under the aspect of a separate
apologetic casuistry dealing with "moral problems" as if
their consideration could quite properly be separated
from the self-understanding that proceeds from the Biblical witness.[11]

Reformation ethical thought was essentially exegetical
in character. The two greatest treatises of Protestant
ethics well illustrate the Protestant principle of *sola
scriptura*: Luther's *Christian Liberty* and Calvin's *Institutes*.[12] The ethical thought of the major Reformers sought
modestly to be no more and hopefully to be little less

than sound Biblical ethics, reappropriated in understandable language and restructured for new historical contexts.
We find no hint of an autonomous discipline of "Christian social ethics" among the Reformers, since these concerns were taken as a matter of course to be legitimate
and necessary aspects of the regular tasks of exegesis and
systematic theology.

The first major Protestant systematic ethics to stand
independent of exegesis was Schleiermacher's *Die christliche Sitte.*[13] The mainstream of nineteenth-century Protestant theology subsequently came to root all ethical
norms in religious experience, historical studies, or idealistic rationalism. In the century following Schleiermacher
this elaboration of apologetic methodologies ultimately
involved a negation of *sola scriptura* as propaedeutic to
ethics. English and American treatises on ethics, thoroughly affected by this bifurcation, also followed the trend
with few exceptions, and today hardly a single major
Protestant ethicist can reasonably claim to be a competent
exegete. However much Scripture may be "used" in an
eisegetical fashion, seldom does it become determinative
for ethical analysis. Upon close inspection we discover a
noticeable disinterest in exegesis and attraction toward
philosophical, systematic, and apologetic theology among
contemporary Protestant ethicists, with Tillich perhaps
leading the way.

Tillich is widely known as one who has determinatively
shaped Protestant ethics with his seminal doctrines of
kairos, theology of culture, and his method of correlating
cultural questions and theological answers. Yet each of
these contributions remains exegetically rootless.

The center of Tillich's ethic, that which he designates
and evokes as "the Protestant principle," is not distinc-

tively Protestant at all, but it is equally a Platonic and a Thomist principle, since it essentially holds that nothing finite is to be identified or confused with the eternal. A distinctively Protestant principle might be *sola scriptura* in methodology or *sola gratia, sola fide* in soteriology, but there is little distinctively Protestant about the assertion of the unsynonymity of God and the world. In his effort to build a Protestant ethic on a principle of negation, Tillich has cultivated a characteristically un-Protestant *Fragestellung* in ethics, however significant it might be for analysis of the human predicament.[14] Tillich's exegetical rootlessness has permitted his use of philosophical categories often to be determinative of the content of his theological affirmations.[15]

How can Protestant thought proceed beyond the Tillich-Niebuhrian preoccupation with the question of estrangement into the affirmation of grace and authenticity? Tillich is consistently clearer about the analysis of human estrangement than the new being. Reconciliation is never a reality, and only grudgingly is it given the status of a possibility. The new being is always remote. This is consistent with his creation gnosticism which boldly argues that "actualized existence is estranged existence,"[16] in contrast to the Biblical affirmation that creation is good, since it is God's. All this can be laid to the door of a persistent exegetical atrophy that fails to perceive that authentic theological freedom is rooted in obedience to the Word. The problem so sharply found in Tillich's ethics, however, may be found in more or less subtle forms in practically every nook and cranny of current Protestant ethics.

It is in full awareness of this hardened and calloused estrangement of ethics and exegesis that we ask how

Bultmann's work might conceivably help bridge the gap. Since ordinarily we do not think of Bultmann as an ethicist, it is surprising that in the very process of the task of faithfully performing his function as an exegete, Bultmann has delivered up some of the most significant formulations for understanding the Christian life that our generation has received. He has simply tried to perform his modest task as a Biblical theologian, letting the chips fall where they may, and where they have fallen is astonishingly relevant for the future of Protestant ethics. Surprisingly enough, the simple task of honest and clear exegesis may be the undiscovered beginning point for contemporary Protestant ethics. From Bultmann's exegesis we may again learn that *sola scriptura* remains the germinating ground to which Protestant ethics must ever return.

3. Having delineated two problems in contemporary ethics associated with the contributions of Reinhold Niebuhr and Paul Tillich, we now come to a third, which is linked with the theological creativity of Karl Barth and Dietrich Bonhoeffer. The uneasiness we feel in this respect is *the hiatus between a high Christology and actual Christian obedience.*

Barth's Christological ethic, centering on the theme of the obedience of Jesus Christ *in our place,* fails to take as seriously as it might the reality and depth of the human predicament, precisely the opposite of Tillich's overwhelming concern. Barth's ethics always runs the danger of abstract idealization of man and history as *de jure* participators in the reality of Christ.[17] However much that word needs to be clarified, it should never lead to an indifference to the concrete tragedy of *de facto* man and history.

Although the Barthian ethic may offer a needed corrective to Tillich and Niebuhr in some respects (especially

their temptation to become preoccupied with the brokenness of man to the neglect of the word of reconciliation),
Barth remains constantly in danger of an archaism in his
hermeneutic and theological language, perceiving less
well than his contemporaries the need for nonreligious
interpretations of Biblical concepts (Bonhoeffer), demythologizing of the kerygma (Bultmann), and correlating theology with the questions of culture (Tillich).
Barth's amazing boredom in the face of the astonishing
creativity of contemporary philosophy, psychotherapy,
existential literature, and art forms witnesses to the atrophy of his desire to communicate with the contemporary
mind. Barth's romance with Mozart[18] is a clue to his
nostalgia for a day gone by and his lack of touch with the
internal reality of the contemporary mind whose nihilism
and cynicism he rejects as empty of significance.[19]

Since Dietrich Bonhoeffer has emerged in the last two
decades as one of the most remarkable thinkers of the
Protestant tradition, it seems salutary to consider how his
contribution relates to the sickness and health of contemporary Protestant ethics. We have every right to consider
Bonhoeffer in the same breath with Barth, since Bonhoeffer is in most essential respects a Barthian who asked
embarrassing questions.[20]

Although Bonhoeffer's ethics runs the same danger we
find in Barth, that of perceiving reality exclusively from
the viewpoint of Jesus Christ and consequently neglecting
the validity of an unchristological *Daseins* analysis,[21] we
can hardly assert that he had no awareness of the human
tragedy since he himself was as deeply implicated in it
as any theologian in the history of the church. His injunc-
tion against "thinking in terms of two spheres" so as to
misplace the reality of God in the world seems to be only

partly defensible, however.[22] For despite his notion of the
penultimate, we can hardly imagine how Bonhoeffer's
ethic could provide a secure theological basis for protecting civil justice against religious fanaticism.[23] To a certain
extent it seems necessary to think in terms of two spheres
in order to protect the Christian community from culture-
Protestant erosion, but such thinking must never eclipse
the church's confession of the freedom of God to share
his life with the world. Niebuhr's inadequacy is exactly
the opposite of Bonhoeffer's. For if Niebuhr does not do
sufficient justice to the self-disclosure of God at the center
of history and consequently in the here and now, Bonhoeffer fails to do sufficient justice to the need for special
knowledge in discriminating moral judgments. Perhaps
the dialectic we find in Luther,[24] slightly oversimplified
by Bonhoeffer, will be useful in teaching us again to
think properly in terms of two spheres without neglecting
either the Lordship of God over the world or the freedom
of the world in the face of the Lordship of God.

If Barth and Bonhoeffer represent only partial achievements in ethics, how might Bultmann's work be a significant corrective of some of their inadequacies? Bonhoeffer's doctrine of "simple obedience" (which Barth
strictly follows)[25] runs the risk of a fanaticism and sub-
jectivism in ethical resolution which is avoided by Bultmann's anthropology (largely shaped by Buber, Heidegger, and Gogarten). In Reinhold Niebuhr and Tillich the
principal concern is for understanding the predicament
of man amid an immoral society, whereas in Barth and
Bonhoeffer the principal concern is toward the man of
faith and the renewing event of God's electing love. In
neither Barth, Bonhoeffer, Tillich, nor Niebuhr, however,
do we find the appropriate balance between both a

Daseins analytic and a kerygmatic theology which we encounter constantly in Bultmann.

Bultmann acts as a corrective both to Barthian temptation toward archaism and to the post-Bonhoefferian temptation toward a dehistoricized ecclesiology. Perhaps the greatest contribution of Bultmann to moral analysis is his capacity to do precisely what Bonhoeffer warned us against, and to do it without injury to the theological process, viz., think in terms of two spheres, not in the semibifurcated sense that Reinhold Niebuhr thinks in two spheres but with a finesse that emerges out of deep immersion in the Lutheran tradition. There are good indications that Bonhoeffer was studying the demythology controversy during the period of his most intense contribution to modern Protestant ethics, viz., his last days in prison. Again this supports our basic contention that Bultmann offers some new keys for the improvement, modification, and elaboration of the current issues in Protestant ethics, now in something of a quandary.

We have attempted to set forth briefly some emerging problems and inadequacies of current Protestant ethics. Although this is little more than a cursory sketch of certain special features of a rich and complex landscape, it may serve to sound an initial note of introduction to Bultmann's ethic by way of indicating its relevance for our present situation.[26]

I

RADICAL OBEDIENCE

R ADICAL OBEDIENCE means *to listen for and respond to the Word of God speaking through the situation in which one exists*. The demand of the moment must be taken with all seriousness as God's own demand.[1]

Such is the core idea with which Bultmann finds the eschatological ethic of the New Testament saturated. The New Testament presupposes that the reign of God is at hand! This immediate expectation of God's imminent coming is the presupposition of the call to obedience in the New Testament. A radical claim is laid upon man because of the emerging reality of God's presently impinging Kingdom.[2]

A. The Demand of the Moment as God's Demand

1. Radical obedience is *an eschatological ethic*.[3] The idea of radical obedience appears nowhere in Bultmann's writings apart from discussions of New Testament and prophetic eschatology. One cannot conceive of obedience in its radical New Testament meaning if one ignores the view of time and history in which this idea had its matrix. If spuriously separated from this eschatological consciousness, it easily becomes quite an artificial moral abstraction.[4]

25

The uniqueness of Jesus' proclamation, in contrast to that of all other apocalyptic preachers, is the *nowness* of God's reign in history. "Now the time is come! The Reign of God is breaking in! The time of the End is here!"[5] It was Jesus' overwhelming conviction that the new age of God's righteousness was not merely ahead, in the distant or near future, but at hand, and impinging *now* upon all things human. This belief, says Bultmann, constitutes the controlling presupposition of Jesus' call for obedience.[6]

This eschatological consciousness carries with it an implicit imperative, which summons men to live now in terms of God's coming reign. It calls men to answer an absolute either/or: either to order their lives in terms of God's new order, or to cling to their former outmoded self-understanding. Whenever the proclamation of God's impinging reign is made, men are called to decision in terms of it, and this imperative is laid upon them. The coming reign of God made the present, as proclaimed by Jesus, a time of radical decision.[7]

Obedience to God in such a context means to be open to the future, since the future belongs to God. The eschatological proclamation announces a new age in history, calling its hearer to abandon the understanding of existence that characterized his past life and live in terms of God's future, which is already breaking into the present.[8]

2. The eschatological and the ethical are as two sides of a coin. Taken in their oneness, they constitute the idea of radical obedience. A central hermeneutic principle in Bultmann's writing is that one must not sever "the unity of the eschatological and the ethical proclamation."[9] *The ethical radicalizes the eschatological. The eschatological provides the context for the ethical.*

In his idea of radical obedience, Bultmann is admittedly

attempting to bring together two divergent schools of New Testament interpretation and correct their inadequacies: on the one hand, the ethical emphasis of the older liberalism that regarded Jesus' teachings as the nucleus of New Testament thought,[10] and on the other hand, the eschatological emphasis of J. Weiss and Albert Schweitzer, who regarded the moral imperatives of Jesus merely as "interim ethic." Bultmann argues, however, that "both the eschatological and the ethical teachings of Jesus belong equally to the oldest stratum of the tradition,"[11] and that the radical nature of Jesus' call to decision and obedience has its ground precisely in the eschatological proclamation.

Jesus' eschatological expectation arose out of the conviction that *God* is the final reality, and that only the future, which belongs to God, can bring salvation. But Jesus is unique in proclaiming that this future faces man in the *present* "and requires of him the decision for the world or for God."[12]

3. The unity of the eschatological and ethical aspects of radical obedience consists of the fact that *the fulfillment of God's will is the condition for participating in God's reign, and yet nothing other than genuine readiness for God's future and God's demand is able to fulfill this condition.* Radical obedience constitutes this readiness, which is the condition for participating in God's reign.[13]

The relation of eschatological and ethical is analogous to the relation of repentance and love. Repentance means turning away from one's former self-understanding, and standing ready for the reign of God. Love, however, is the attitude and activity that characterizes one who is genuinely repentant, i.e., one who stands in genuine readiness for God's future. Only he who *loves* really takes the eschatological proclamation seriously. He is not *ready* for God's reign who does not decide "in the concrete moment for God's demand which meets him in the neighbor."[14] The love of the neighbor is not something that one does merely to take up time while awaiting God's reign. On the contrary, love of the neighbor constitutes readiness for God's future and is the content of radical obedience.[15]

Jesus proclaimed the end time as present and therefore called men to live *as if* the end time were present. "End" is not understood in terms of a chronological end. Jesus' proclamation did not so much concern the end of world history as it did the end of a false understanding of ourselves and history, which lives on the illusion that God's sovereignty is not present in time. End time must be understood in the sense of the *final* time—the time of ultimate judgment and decision.

B. The Proclamation of Jesus

1. The ethics of Jesus centers in the idea of *obedience*, like all Jewish ethics; but in contrast to the legalism of late Judaism, Jesus "conceived the idea of obedience radically."[16] Radical obedience means, *in nuce*, to understand the demand of the moment as God's demand, and to answer it as such with one's total being and doing.[17]

It is in connection with the proclamation of Jesus that Bultmann most clearly explicates the notion of radical obedience. Jesus lived and taught as a Jewish rabbi. Jesus' demand for radical obedience must be viewed as a renewal of the prophetic tradition and a protest against Pharisaic legalism.[18]

In late Judaic legalism a formal concept of obedience prevailed which assumed that the commandments were to be obeyed simply because they had been commanded.[19] Although the law had largely lost its original meaning as an expression of the covenant relation, the legal codes had been preserved and sanctified by the authority of tradition. Bultmann terms this *formal obedience,* since the law had lost its content but its form remained. Jesus repudiated formal obedience of Pharisaic legalism in his call to radical obedience.

In formal obedience there is no claim upon the total man in all his being and doing, but rather merely a claim upon certain of his external actions.[20] The fundamental aim of the formally obedient man is to do the commands of the sacred law without reference either to the being of the doer or to the content of the law. Bultmann contrasts formal obedience of late Jewish legalism with the prophetic idea of obedience in which the whole man was addressed by the gift and demand of the covenant God, and in which the content of man's action was the keen concern rather than the mere formal fact of his obedience to the law.[21]

2. The most important consequence of the formal idea of obedience was that it led to the seeking of merit, or to making claims upon God. *When the law is regarded as clearly identifiable in a number of statutes, the temptation of the religious man is to strive to go beyond the requirement of the law and accumulate merit before God.* The law, when regarded as captured in written codes, can never embrace every conceivable situation, since each moment is unique and singular. So long as there are occasions in life that are allegedly free (directly or indirectly) from God's claim, there can be no radical obedience. "For in radical obedience man knows himself to be addressed by God in the totality of his being and in all situations."[22]

The characteristic feature of legalistic obedience is that the demands of God are specifically known in the plethora of laws, and that the obedient man might legitimately endeavor to win God's favor by minutely fulfilling each statutory stipulation. According to Bultmann, this essentially reflects man's *hubris*, desiring to secure his own future by placing a special claim upon God.[23] Under these conditions, no matter how trivial the requirement, it was obeyed because it was required, in the hope that one might be found meritorious before God.[24]

The proclamation of Jesus, in contrast, represents a renewal of the prophetic tradition in terms of which man knows God's will by *hearing*. Unlike the Greek world, which constantly used the analogy of *seeing*, the Bible relies for moral knowledge upon the analogy of hearing and answering.[25] The will of God is to be apprehended by hearing in the midst of the self's encounter with life. Knowledge of God's will has nothing to do with his metaphysical nature, but solely with listening to his demand. Therefore the hearing of God's demand can never become an abstract science separated from the demand of the moment! For this reason no system of ethics can be derived from the Biblical witness, but only the demand to be radically obedient to God in the moment.[26]

3. *Radical obedience is therefore not a "work" in the sense of an activity in which the self does not fully participate, but rather must be understood as one's deed, i.e., an act in which one's whole being participates in one's doing.*

Radical obedience is present only when a man inwardly affirms what is required of him, when the requirement is understood as God's demand; or better, when the whole man is *in* what he does, when he is not doing something obediently, but *is* obedient in his being.[27]

The distinction that Bultmann makes between deed and work (*Tat und Werk*) is fundamental to the idea of radical obedience.[28]

The less obedience is a work, Bultmann says, the more it is a deed. In a *work*, the self goes alongside the doing, or places it outside of itself. In doing a work the self can stand back and look at it, assess it, criticize it, or be proud of it. But in doing a *deed*, the self finds itself in the midst of the doing. One becomes something new in the deed, expressing his very being in his doing. In contrast to a work, in the deed one cannot stand apart from his act, isolate himself from it, assess and review it.[29]

In the Greek concept of work (*ergon*), the self can objectify its action. Its work is something apart from itself, and thus one may see it as an object.[30] But the Hebrew understanding of being and doing suggests that man's being exists through his doing. Man chooses himself in his action. Therefore in the moment of obedience the self cannot judge itself as either obedient or disobedient. The instant I seek to look at myself and evaluate myself in my action, the nature of the act as an obedient act is already destroyed and the action becomes merely a judgment about myself already objectified.[31]

4. Another necessary presupposition, without which the ethic of radical obedience would be unable to function, is the notion of *the discernibility (Einsichtigkeit) of the demand of God in the moment. Einsicht* means insight; if something is *einsichtig,* one may have insight into it; it is discernible, perceptible. *Einsichtigkeit* means having the quality of discernibility, or that into which one may have insight. Unfortunately, the rendering given this term in the English translation, "intelligibility," connotes an abstract direction away from the concreteness of the moment. Bultmann does not mean to say that one may by rational analysis grasp the command of God in a particular situation, but rather that the demand of God is written

into the situation in such a way that in itself it is not obscure, but clear and discernible. Insofar as we do not hear it, the fault lies in our hearing, not in the command itself.[32]

One might say that the demand of God is "hearable," following the Biblical analogy, that one hears rather than sees the will of God. It is assumed in the Old Testament that men know of God's will only because God has spoken to them, and thereby made himself known. To *see* God's will, if that is conceivable, would be to visualize and reason about it prior to the moment of action, and if that were possible, it could be organized into a systematic presentation. But the Hebrew had no word for "visible," and the notion of getting possession or control of God's will was incredible to him. Man hears God's Word only because God speaks to him in the situation in which he exists. The notion that there could be a situation for which God had no will, or in which God did not have anything to say to man, was unthinkable to the Hebrew.[33]

The parable of the good Samaritan illustrates that the demand of God is clear. The priest and the Levite meet the beaten man on the side of the road. They are unmistakably confronted with what they *ought* to do. It is clear. The demand of the moment is discernible. But although squarely confronted by the special demand of the moment, they do not really hear it as the demand of God. They merely pass by the beaten man, as if to say that the demand of the neighbor in need is not the demand of God, but rather something infinitely less important. The Samaritan comes upon the scene and is confronted by the same demand, which is discernible to him as it was to the priest and Levite. The only difference is that the demand of the moment (which has always had the character of discernibility) is now answered with one's total being and doing as God's demand.[34]

5. We have seen that radical obedience is characterized first by the full participation of one's being in one's doing, and secondly by the idea of the discernibility of the demand of the moment. Another feature of radical obedience is that *the self cannot bring with it into the present any standard of action from the past.*

Man cannot meet the crisis of real decision armed with a definite standard or ideal of action. Thus many of the most cherished notions of ethics are found by Bultmann to be quite useless. The notions that we can habituate the self toward good action, that we can enter the situation with a law that tells us what to do, or that we can determine prior to the moment anything about the demand of the moment, all are rejected by Bultmann. All these ways of ethical reflection, he says, seek to lay hold of man's possibilities, domesticate them, and bring them under rational control. They flee from the demand of the moment in an effort to prescribe previously what the moment shall demand. Thus, each one of them is contrary to radical obedience, in which man does not seek lordship over the present, but allows the present moment to be his commander.[35]

He who radically obeys the demand of the moment stands completely insecure before the possibilities that confront him, yet in faith he is open to these possibilities. He does not flee from this standardlessness of the moment, but hearkens to it and allows the moment to create its own demand. He seeks to put neither the present nor the future under spurious bondage to ethical systems but, rather, allows the moment to speak its own unique word of claim.[36]

C. What the Moment Demands

If radical obedience consists essentially in regarding the demand of the moment as the demand of God, then one may ask precisely *what* the moment demands.

1. The first thing Bultmann says in response to such a question is that we cannot anticipate what the moment demands prior to the moment. It is the nature of the moment to create its own unique demands. The demand of God must be perceived in the moment, rather than in principles or laws of conduct abstracted from the moment.[37]

The moment contains *all* that is necessary for understanding the will of God. All the standards that are brought *to* the moment out of the past are called radically into question by the moment.[38] All ethical principles are placed in the category of the problematic in one's concrete encounter with the neighbor and the moment.

All continuity with the past is broken, Bultmann says, and there is no durable standard available "out of the past or out of the general."[39] Human decision, and therefore obedience, cannot take place in a past moment. *Now* is the only moment in which one decides.

Man is not and cannot be the measurer of what the moment demands. He has no measuring stick to bring to the moment. Rather, the uniqueness of the moment with its particular demands is the measurer of man. The moment lays its demand upon man and calls man to answer it even in all its uniqueness.

The standardlessness of man in the face of the moment does not mean, however, that decision is made without insight or without knowledge of prior things and consequent things. On the contrary, Bultmann argues that what the moment demands always becomes clearer with a practical knowledge of precedents and consequents. But decision that takes place in one's actual meeting of his neighbor in the moment is never determined by such knowledge.[40]

This does not mean that man never knows what he ought to do. On the contrary, Bultmann is persistent in saying that the moment clearly teaches man what is morally good. Man knows what he ought to do, not out of rational analysis or education or past experience, but directly "out of the situation of the Now."[41] *The content of the morally good action cannot be known until it is revealed or disclosed in the situation.* The situation is the teacher.[42]

2. *It is only in direct encounter with the neighbor that man discovers what he must do* in radical obedience to God. If the self is abstracted out of its encounter with the neighbor and considered nonhistorically, nothing can be said about the content of radical obedience. In the situation of concrete encounter with the neighbor, however, man is trusted and expected to know what he ought to do. The demand of God is not obscure and ambiguous but revealed and clarified by the need of the neighbor.

What the will of God is, is not declared by an external authority in such a way that the content of the command is a matter of indifference, but man is trusted and counted upon to see for himself what is demanded of him. The requirements of God intend to be discernible.[43]

What does the moment demand? It does not demand a *what* but a *that.*[44] It demands, in every conceivable situation, *that we love.* But the *content* (the specific "what") of this love must be left to the existing individual in his concrete situation.[45]

The parable of the talents is used by Bultmann to illustrate that the command of God does not require a *what* (a specific content to human action), but rather a *that*. The parable charges the hearer with responsible use of the gifts of God. It allows him, however, to choose how he specifically is to be responsible. It tells him *that* he must be responsible, not *what* specifically he must do in order to be responsible. It is in this sense that Bultmann regards the command of God as *formal*. "The great command to love says nothing concerning the *content* of love," Bultmann declares.[46]

What the moment demands is always *that* we love our neighbor as ourselves. The command itself does not and cannot undertake the burden of deciding *what* it means to love the neighbor in every conceivable situation. But Bultmann is consistently confident that the particular content which love shall take is always unambiguous in the moment of concrete encounter as in the case of the good Samaritan.[47]

The demand for love needs no formulated stipulations; the example of the merciful Samaritan shows that a man can know and must know what he has to do when he sees his neighbor in need of his help. The little words "as yourself" in the love-commandment pre-indicate both the boundlessness and the direction of loving conduct. Jesus completely refrained from making the love-commandment concrete in specific prescriptions.[48]

3. Everyone *knows* how to love his neighbor, Bultmann suggests, because he knows how he himself would wish to be loved. The commandment merely serves the purpose of pointing out to man that he ought to love his neighbor as himself. It does not tell him what to do in order to love his neighbor, since he already knows that, by virtue of

knowing what he would wish others to do on his behalf.[49] The phrase "as thyself" is the key to the *content* of the demand of God in the moment.

The command to love is formal, and yet loving the neighbor is never without concreteness, for it never exists apart from some special situation in which it is clear that one should love his neighbor as himself. Man never knows the specific content of love prior to the point at which he sees his neighbor in need. Then he can and must know.[50]

If one asks, "What should I do when conflicts of values arise?" or, "What ought I do when I have two different neighbors to love and these duties clash?" he may find a concise answer in the phrase "as thyself."[51] This phrase clarifies the extent of *what* a man ought to do to love in every conceivable situation, since every man loves himself and therefore clearly knows how he wishes to be loved. "As thyself" does not tell us what love is, but it shows us that no man can plead ignorance before the command to love or claim that the demand of God is ambiguous.[52]

The phrase "as thyself" does not define what love is, but it does make the questioner aware that he does not know what love is because he does not love. He who loves does not ask to know what love is. One only knows what love is by loving.[53] He who asks what love is does not understand this paradox, says Bultmann. The question is a loveless question.

This paradox is what Bultmann calls the *hiddenness*[54] of Christian love. A loving act can never be proved to be a loving act to one who is unloving. If the meaning of love is known only in the unique situation in which one actually loves his neighbor, then one can never stand back

from the act of loving the neighbor and congratulate oneself that he has loved. Love has no time to report on
itself.[55]

4. The twofold command to love God and love the
neighbor is regarded by Bultmann as a double way of
saying a single thing. Neither command is derived from
the other and they belong together. Only that obedience
which lives in the concrete meeting with the neighbor
can be obedience to God. The first commandment points
toward the second, and the second specifies the meaning
of the first. To love God means precisely to renounce one's
claims upon one's neighbor and stand ready to serve him.
To love the neighbor means nothing other than to obey
the demand of God in the situation in which the neighbor
confronts me.[56]

The elusive question we have been pursuing is, "What
does the moment demand?" Bultmann stakes his whole
answer to this question on the command to love God and
to love one's neighbor as oneself. *Although the command
is a formal statement of what ought to be done, the actual
deed of loving the neighbor is always the unique content
of the calling of the moment.*

The readiness to forgive without limit, the giving of a
cup of cold water to a thirsty man, visiting those in prison,
avoiding envy and anger, and helping the fatherless and
defenseless may be marks of love of the neighbor. Such
actions may tell us who one is who is radically obedient
to God. But they grow out of love, instead of love being
produced by them. They cannot be arranged in an order
of priority. Even if codified, they cannot ensure love.

Whoever continues legalistically to pursue the question,
"What, then, am I to do?" seeking for specific counsel
on the content of the command to love, has never stopped

to hear the call of the neighbor in the moment. We have pursued the matter as far as we can. There is nothing more *in particular*, according to Bultmann, to say about *what* the moment demands.[57]

5. Love is not sympathy. Love is not synonymous with a feeling of admiration for the neighbor, or approval or disapproval of his condition.[58] Love is consequently not an emotion, or an affection of a certain strength competing with other affections of other strengths. If everything depended upon a feeling of sympathy, the standard of preference would have its locus within the emotive self rather than in the neighbor's need. One's inclination, passion, or appetite, rather than the demand of the moment, would then become the final arbiter of action. Behavior would be shaped finally by one's own feelings of compassion (or lack of them) rather than by the need of the neighbor that confronts one from without. Consequently Bultmann rejects the ethics of sympathy as being ultimately rooted in self-interest.[59]

In this respect Bultmann clearly maintains the Kantian dictum that the basis of moral action cannot be within the inclinations or emotive functions of man. If love is based on sympathy, one's feelings about the neighbor may come to play a greater role than the neighbor's objective need.

To put the issue sharply, love does not depend on man's feeling but on God's command. The command of God is discernible *only* in the moment of meeting with the neighbor. Love is not a feeling of the individuated self, but is a way of relating oneself to other men, viz., by regarding the demand of the moment of encounter with the neighbor as the demand of God.[60]

Love, therefore, is what the moment demands. It "shows

how obedience can be practiced in the concrete situation
in which man exists with other men."[61] One does not love
the neighbor out of sympathy or emotional correspondence with his situation, nor because of his human worth
as a rational being, nor because there are certain goods
or values that he wishes to uphold, nor because he is seeking to be virtuous, nor because love is the absolute value
among relative values, nor because love is a high ideal
of human conduct, but rather because the neighbor is
in need and his need constitutes the demand of God in
any moment.

The neighbor is not the man for whom one feels sympathy, nor the man one might pick out as the most needy.
It is every man, says Bultmann, yet not every man in
general, but every man who meets me in the moment with
a concrete need. Every moment, of course, is such a
moment.[62]

In this way Bultmann's concept of radical obedience
is given a certain kind of content in the love of the neighbor. The self stands in an immediate relationship to the
command of God, which lays its claim *in concreto* in the
encounter with the neighbor and yet may be stated formally in the command to love the neighbor as thyself.
This is what the moment demands.

D. Radical Obedience as a Concrete Relation

1. *Radical obedience to God cannot be the basis for a
systematic theory of ethics since it refers to a concrete
relation to existence.* In speaking of "the ethics of radical
obedience," we must constantly qualify it by identifying
it as a particular way of deciding but not as a comprehen-
sive systematization of ethics. Radical obedience may be
conceptualized, but in the process it loses the concrete-

ness, historicity, and existentiality that distinguish it from other ethics. In this analysis, of course, we have conceptualized and stated it as systematically as possible, in order to deal with it at all as a particular understanding of the Christian life. But in doing so, we must take care to distinguish concrete radical obedience from its conceptualization. This is the special perplexity of dealing with radical obedience as a proposal for Christian ethics.

"Jesus taught no general ethics," declares Bultmann, insofar as ethics is understood as "a generally intelligible theory for men concerning what one should and should not do."[63] Systematic ethics can be organized only on the basis of an anthropology that understands human "nature" as possessing certain constants that may be relied upon in any given situation. Such ethics seeks to anticipate and reflect upon man's response to various situations in the light of these constants. Radical obedience, on the contrary, is an existential relation in the moment. It does not reach for an interpretation of the demand of any future moment, and therefore resists systematization. It tends to be an ethic against ethics, much in the same way that existentialism has been described as a philosophy against philosophy.[64]

2. This special problem arises directly from Bultmann's Heideggerian presupposition that *man's being is a possibility of being* (*Sein ist ein Seinkönnen*).[65] Human existence (*Dasein*) is not a static being with a fixed "nature," but a being constantly choosing itself. It is a special feature of the ontology of man that he is always in the midst of *choosing who he is.*

Man is always in the state of living toward some goal, but the goal toward which man's life may be oriented is left undetermined by the nature of man or in the formal

ontological structure of his existence.[66] This ontological
structure does, however, offer the possibility of choosing
one's goal. In the midst of this continual choosing of oneself, the self is always involved in the *risk* of gaining or
losing its authentic selfhood.[67]

Thus the being of man is characterized by the exercise
of man's capacity continually to project himself into a
possibility that lies before him. Man is constantly called
to decisions in which he himself is at stake. He is forever
confronted with a future in which he faces the possibility
of gaining or losing authentic life.

In the Gospel of John, e.g., man's fallenness consists in
that he flees from the possibility of choosing himself. He
despairs of his freedom. To cling to one's fallen being
means to surrender one's own possibility of being. That
man has possibilities, no one would dispute, but in his
fallenness he forgets that he himself *is* a possibility of
being, i.e., he ignores the fact that he can either choose to
be himself or reject himself as one who is finitely free.

"The world"[68] can know its fallenness only when revelation speaks to it, since it is the special character of man's
fallenness to be blind to his fallenness. Encountering revelation, man is confronted with two possibilities: either to
cling to his fallenness or to receive God's future. "The
world" turns away from making this decision, but in doing
so, it already decides against itself as a possibility of being
itself. Therefore, man in his fallenness cuts himself off
from his future. To make the decision of faith is to decide
to have a future, to decide to trust that the future belongs
to God.

Thus the special feature of radical obedience is also its
special problem as a theory of ethics. It cannot generalize
in abstraction from the moment. Rather, it can only point

to the demand of the moment. Since the self is always choosing itself, there is no point at which the philosopher can lay hold of the self, take it out of history and decision, look at it timelessly and say, "This is what man's *nature* is and what can be expected of it."[69] The demand of God is never separable from the particular situation in which man is called to choose himself.

3. The obedient man stands constantly ready to become a new self. He does not have a preconceived picture of his true self from which he cannot deviate in the situation of decision. He stands ready to admit that *he does not have final knowledge of what his true selfhood is but that on the contrary he is constantly ready to learn of it anew.*

To be radically obedient to the demand of the moment means to stand open to one's *destiny*. It means to be ready constantly to perish as the old man in order to become a new man. "Death and becoming," says Bultmann, is the only law of the obedient life.[70] The self constantly allows itself to be created anew by God. Every moment is to be embraced as a new creation, unique and unrepeatable in every dimension. Authentic selfhood does not mean that the self has constructed a "true" picture of itself, or imaginatively captured its true destiny in the future, or determined who the true "I" is prior to the moment. Rather, it means to be open always to the possibilities offered in life for the constant re-creation of the self.[71]

4. *Consequently, radical obedience is not a particular view of the world* (*Weltanschauung*). A *world view* is defined by Bultmann as a theory about the world and about life, its unity, origin, purpose, and meaning, in terms of which the self finds security.[72] A world view provides a *general* perspective on life into which man can "fit" as

a particular *case*. Thereby a world view helps man to escape from the enigma that characterizes human existence, which consists of the fact that man is always choosing himself.[73]

A world view regards the concrete moment as an *instance* of a general rule. Therefore, radical obedience stands in sharpest contrast to any world view, since its unique feature is to allow the moment to legislate its own unique demand, rather than to fit the moment into a general pattern of a preconceived moral system. The moment, according to Bultmann, can never be an instance of a general rule, or an aspect of a general theory about life's meaning, since every moment is filled to the brim with uniqueness.[74]

Radical obedience cannot be learned in an educational process or "retained in the form of a proposition."[75] It is born only of the moment. It operates on the assumption that "what man has done and does in his decisions constitute *him* in his true nature."[76] A *world view*, in contrast, decides what man is in his "true nature" prior to his decision.

5. *Bultmann sharply distinguishes radical obedience from all types of perfectionist, humanist, idealistic, and value theories of ethics.* In all these views he perceives one controlling presupposition operative: that man is essentially in control of his future and his possibilities for self-fulfillment.

Bultmann interprets the whole tradition of Greek ethics (the spring from which most of the moral philosophies of the West have drunk) as operating essentially out of this presupposition, understanding moral action generally by the analogy of the artist or craftsman, in which the artisan employs *technē* to shape material to its ideal condition, or *telos*. The Greeks conceived of the idea of obedience under the general notion of *paideia*—the shaping of the self in education. The Biblical view stands in contrast to this with its understanding of the concrete I-Thou dialogue with God and the neighbor as the controlling image for understanding life's task.

The Greek felt himself called to obey not the demand of a neighbor in need but an *idea*, such as fortitude or prudence. The task of the rational self was to shape itself to the ideal condition proposed. Consequently the self sought to embody within itself these ideal qualities or excellent modes of action, such as loyalty, temperance, and justice.[77]

Any ethical theory that revolves around the idea of *development* toward an *ideal* must stand in strict contrast to the ethics of radical obedience. Likewise any ethics in which man is regarded as being endowed with a predetermined *telos*, and as being able, by the habitual training of his will to nurture certain modes of excellent activity by which he may actualize the unique human purpose as prescribed by his "nature," presupposes a world view contrary to the ethics of radical obedience. For radical obedience rejects the presupposition that man can domesticate his future.[78]

Since the notion of radical obedience operates out of an existentialist view of man and an eschatological view of history, it contains an implicit rejection of any ethics that tries to understand man apart from his concrete encounter with the moment. This is its distinctive feature and its distinctive problem as a proposal for Christian ethics.

II

EXISTENTIAL ANALYSIS OF HUMAN OBLIGATION

IN HIS ESSAY on "Bultmann's Project of Demythologization and the Problem of Theology and Philosophy,"[1] Schubert M. Ogden contends that the central issue Bultmann raises for contemporary theology is the relation of theology and philosophy. He argues that although Bultmann intends to distinguish between theology and philosophy, there is real doubt as to whether he actually does in a clear way. "He both denies and affirms the ultimate identity of theology and philosophy."[2] Contrary to Bultmann, Ogden asserts that Christian existence is an original actualizable possibility of man as such apart from the address of the Christian kerygma, and that Bultmann's attempt to distinguish between theology and philosophy is "hopelessly self-contradictory," since it rests on the "specious distinction" between a possibility in principle and a possibility in fact.[3]

In contrast to Ogden's analysis, we will maintain in this chapter that Bultmann's distinction can and should be maintained. In fact, we will proceed to set forth the distinction between ontological and ontic possibility as the irreplaceable key to Bultmann's ethical analysis.

This chapter and the one following constitute the heart

of our study in Bultmann's ethics. This chapter will engage in an existential analysis of *man as such* as a being under requirement. The following chapter will inquire into the address of the *Christian proclamation* offering man a new and actual possibility of authentic life, radically transforming the ethical possibilities of the natural man. Thus we are, in contrast to Ogden's analysis, deliberately separating Bultmann's philosophical and theological analyses into two chapters. As we proceed, it will become increasingly clear how these two dimensions relate to and supplement each other, but it will be maintained that they may be legitimately distinguished.

Bultmann's theological program has two sides, the negative side of demythologization and the positive side of existential analysis of the Christian proclamation.[4] Although much of the discussion following Bultmann has centered on the question of demythologizing, and although we remain peripherally interested in this problem in this study, our keener interest is with the positive side of Bultmann's efforts to develop an existential analysis of the ontology of man as a being under requirement. Demythologization is distinguished from existential analysis (*Daseinsanalyse*) in that the former deals with the special problem of trying to perceive the New Testament proclamation in the context of the mythical world picture of the first century, and to indicate how this world picture is not necessary to the particular understanding of existence expressed therein. Existential analysis of the New Testament proclamation, however, involves the positive task of taking these first-century conceptualities, language, and meanings and translating them into terms that are familiar and understandable to modern man and that correspond to the actual situation of human existence. However in-

teresting the debate over demythologization remains, we
are here more concerned with existential analysis, since it
is in this connection that Bultmann deals more directly
with the issue of natural moral knowledge.

The central question with which we launch into this
discussion is none other than the core issue that lies between Kantian and Biblical views of obedience, viz.,
whether the ground of moral obligation is resident within
the self, or whether it confronts the self as distinctly
"other" than the self.[5]

A. ONTOLOGICAL AND ONTIC MORAL POSSIBILITIES OF MAN

1. As early as 1929, Gerhardt Kuhlmann charged that,
since the method of a science is determined by its object,
and since the object of Heidegger's existential analysis is
not the "believing" man but the "natural" man, Bultmann's
use of Heidegger amounts to a profanization and falsifica-
tion of revelation.[6] Bultmann's answer to this charge in
1930 in the article "The Historicity of Man and Faith"[7]
constitutes one of the most important works pertaining to
our inquiry.

Although he concurred with Kuhlmann that theological
method is indissolubly related to its object, Bultmann took
the position that the special object of existential analysis
is human existence (*Dasein*). *Since the man of faith remains man even amid his renewed self-understanding, it
is necessary for theology to inquire into and understand
man as such.* Admittedly, natural man is the theme of
philosophy, whereas believing man is the theme of theology. Both of them, however, deal with *man,* and thus
existential analysis[8] is appropriate to both.

2. *Philosophy cannot take into consideration, however,
the special presupposition which makes theology a dis-*

tinctive science, viz., that the Christian proclamation addresses the existing individual concerning the deed of God.[9] Philosophy does not have this character of address. Philosophy has the character of analysis of the formal possibilities of human existence. If it should take on the character of address, it would cease to be philosophy and become proclamation. The task of philosophy, on the contrary, is to inquire strictly into the formal ontological structure of man, rather than proclaim a definite word to man's concrete situation.

Nevertheless the task of theology remains closely related to that of philosophy. For since the existence of the man of faith does not cease to be human existence, it is appropriate that the self-understanding of the man of faith come under the purview of existential analysis.[10] Furthermore, since the Christian proclamation addresses the existing individual as a human word cast into a particular historical and existential context, it is fitting that the self-understanding that arises from this proclamation submit to existential analysis.

3. Bultmann makes a crucial distinction between man's *ontological possibility* and his *ontic* possibility for authentic life,[11] which upon careful inspection appears to be determinative for Bultmann's ethics and forms the whole basis for the ensuing discussion.

If we inquire adequately into the ontology of man (man's particular way of being in the world), we learn that man's being is a possibility of being,[12] i.e., man is that being who is constantly choosing who he *is*. Therefore man is unavoidably involved in a relation with himself. In the midst of his choosing of who he shall be, he is in every moment faced with two fundamental alternatives. Either he may understand himself in such a way as to deny spuriously the fact of his self-relation by closing himself against his future possibilities; or he can understand himself in such a way as to remain open to these possibilities and in doing so preserve his original relation to himself.[13]

Man's formal possibility for authentic life can be adequately described apart from the address of Christian proclamation. The philosopher without the kerygma can *conceive* of this possibility through existential analysis. Since this possibility belongs formally to the ontology of every man, Bultmann speaks of it as man's *ontological possibility* for authentic life.[14]

The situation of man as it is expressed in the New Testament, however, is such that man has always already *lost* this possibility in his actual existence. This is the central meaning of the New Testament presupposition that man is under bondage to *sin.* Although the New Testament objectifies this power as if it were outside the self, laying hold upon man as an alien force, Bultmann believes that its understanding of human existence is quite consonant with the existential interpretation of man as having already lost his original formal possibility for authentic life.[15] By means of demonic imagery, the New Testament expresses in a mythological fashion the existentialist insight that man is alienated from himself in actuality, however much authentic life may remain formally within the range of describable human possibilities.

The Christian proclamation addresses the existing individual amid his situation of bondage (sin) and offers him a new and actual possibility of authentic existence. Only the Christian proclamation knows of the deed of God that makes possible acceptance of one's past (forgiveness) and openness to the future (faith), which constitute authentic human existence. *It is only when man is addressed by the Christian proclamation that authentic existence becomes an actual possibility rather than merely a formally describable possibility that is always already lost in actual existence.* This is what Bultmann terms man's *ontic possibility* for authenticity. "Ontic" refers to the actual (*existenziell!*) situation of the being of a particular man, in contrast to the formal (ontological) structures of his being.

Man's *existenziell* situation, man's concrete encounter with this moment of existence, is to be distinguished from the *existential analysis* of which we have been speaking. John Macquarrie makes the following distinction between "what are termed *existentiell* (*existenziell*) and 'existential' (*existenzial*) possibilities. The concrete practical possibilities of the individual *Dasein* are his *existentiell* possibilities. But there are horizons to *Dasein's* possibilities—limits within which every individual existence must fall. These wide possibilities are called existential, and their investigation is the subject of the existential analytic of *Dasein*."[16] Macquarrie notes that the term "existential" is not an attempt to describe "universal properties" of *Dasein,* since man is not an object, but an attempt to show "the horizons of possibility within which the concrete possibilities of every individual *Dasein* must fall." This interpretation seems appropriate to Bultmann's usage of the terms.

In summary, an acknowledgment of sin and forgiveness, and therefore the possibility of authentic life, is an actual *ontic* possibility only in the context of the Christian proclamation. But as a formal possibility of the ontological structure of man, authentic existence may be explicated clearly by the philosopher. The philosopher, however, can speak only of a "possibility in principle," or of an *onto-logical* possibility, whereas the Christian proclamation addresses man with such a *possibility in fact*. Although theology is thereby distinguished from existential analysis, it should be willing to learn about the phenomenon *Dasein* with which both philosopher and theologian deal. Christian existence remains subject to existential analysis since the man of faith does not cease to be man. The authentic life that it proclaims can be explicated as within the range of human possibilities by philosophical analysis, but not actualized. Put in a single phrase, *authentic life may be adequately conceptualized by philosophy as a formal ontological "possibility in principle" through existential analysis, but is actualizable as an ontic "possibility in fact" only under the address of the Christian proclamation to man in his existentiell situation.*[17]

Ogden suggests that this distinction between ontological and ontic possibilities merely restates the difficulty of trying both to affirm and deny the ultimate unity of philosophy and theology, for if man has always already lost this possibility as he actually exists, then it is no longer a possibility of any kind.[18] Thus he regards Bultmann as "hopelessly self-contradictory" at this point. From our point of view, however, there seems nothing unreasonable in conceiving of and describing a possibility that cannot (under certain circumstances, viz., man's sin) be actualized. A psychotherapist, for example, could describe the theoretical possibility of self-acceptance to a depressed patient who could not under his present neurotic circumstances actualize that possibility.

4. The same distinction is found in Paul's usage of the concept *sōma* (body) in which the whole person is able to come under the dominion of powers outside the self. The starting point of Bultmann's existential analysis of

sōma is again man's unavoidable relation with himself.[19] Since man is man (with this particular faculty of self-relation), he constantly relates himself to himself in either an appropriate or perverted way.[20] Man does not "have" *sōma;* he "is" *sōma.* He exists as a man with the formal possibilities of authentic self-relatedness or self-estrangement.[21] It is part of the formal ontological structure of human existence that man is given the possibility (in principle) of being at one with himself as well as the possibility (in principle) of estrangement from himself.[22]

Given this ontological structure, man is always living *toward* some goal. Man lives in his *intentionality.* His existence is always a movement toward purposes through which he hopes to actualize his authentic existence.[23] The fact that men always live toward some goal is a neutral aspect of the ontology of man and neither morally good nor bad. Man's obedience or disobedience does not lie in the fact *that* he chooses goals but rather has to do with the more fundamental question of whether one is living out of a perverted or authentic intentionality.[24]

The end toward which the self is oriented is left quite undetermined in the ontological structure of intentional human existence; but this structure provides the possibility of choosing one's goals, of decision for good or bad, for or against God.[25]

Thus, living is like *walking (peripateō),* since human existence is constantly "on the move," projecting itself into possibilities in terms of which it hopes to gain authentic life *(zōē).*[26] But the future that lies before man always carries the real possibilities of either gaining or losing oneself. Obedience to God involves constantly giving up the illusion that one can gain authentic life on his own by securing his future against possibilities.

A similar view is found in the New Testament understanding of the heart (*kardia*), that aspect of man's being
which intends, strives, purposes, desires, and loves. Man
"sets his heart" on goals through which he would fain
achieve authentic life.[27] But in his situation of alienation
from himself man always already has missed the goal of
authentic life that he at heart seeks. This is likewise expressed in the New Testament understanding of "living
according to the flesh" (*sarx*). *Man according to the flesh
aims at authentic life but always already stands in a false
relation to himself that causes him to pervert his original
intention.*[28] Evil is nothing other than this: a perverted
intentionality.[29] The willing of self-assertive man is always
deflected away from his fundamental intention because
he already "lives from and toward himself and the world"
rather than from and toward God.[30] Bultmann summarily
says:

> The sinful self-delusion that one gains life out of the created
> order can manifest itself both in an unthinking carelessness
> (this especially among the gentiles), and in over-serious
> works-righteousness (this especially among the Jews). It can
> manifest itself either in ignoring ethical demands or in exces-
> sive zeal to fulfill them. The sphere of *sarx* (the flesh) is by
> no means just the life of instinct or sensual passions, but it is
> just as much that of the moral and religious endeavors of
> man.[31]

5. Why is it that man intends to achieve authentic life
but does not achieve it? Bultmann's clearest answer is
found in his exegesis of Rom., ch. 7. Here again he makes
decisive use of the distinction between the ontological
and ontic possibilities of man.

When Paul speaks of "the law of my *nous*" (mind or
understanding), he is speaking of the ontological possi-

bility (or possibility in principle) of man to aim for authentic life. The heart of man's predicament, however, is that although it belongs to the ontology of man to aim at the good, nevertheless man's *doing* is always frustrated by an inauthentic relation to existence.[32] This is the factual or ontic situation of man prior to faith. He strives out of a perverted intentionality.[33]

In his formal ontological structure man has both the possibility of aiming at the good and the possibility of aiming at evil, but these are describable merely as "possibilities in principle." In man's ontic situation, as it is understood in the New Testament, he inevitably fails to actualize this possibility for authentic life because his original intention is perverted by guilt for the past, dread of the future, and pride over his own achievements.[34]

In Rom., ch. 7, Paul unfolds the contradiction between what a man fundamentally intends and what he actually does, when he says "I can will what is right, but I cannot do it." Here the will that wills what is right is not man's actual will (*faktisches Wollen*), says Bultmann, but the fundamental intention (*Grundintention*) of man for authentic life.[35] If this fundamental intention is incapable of realization, it means that the actual will "cannot in fact will what it really wills"![36] What is needed in the will is an acknowledgment of its own utter impotence, so that before it can take seriously the word of grace it must cry: "O wretched man that I am! Who shall deliver me from the body of this death!"

It is in this contradiction between the ontological and ontic possibilities of the will that Paul says, "I do not do what I want, but I do the very thing I hate. . . . The evil I do not want is what I do."[37] It is thus within the range of possibilities formally present to the self to "delight in

the law of God." But in his ontic fallenness man is at war
with this original possibility, or, as Paul says, the law of
my members is in conflict with the law of my understanding.

6. Consistent with this distinction Bultmann asserts that
philosophy oversteps its boundaries if it attempts to
answer *in concreto*, "What ought I to do?" since *the fundamental vocation of all philosophical inquiry is to ask about
the formal possibilities of man.*[38] He does not hide his
admiration for Kant, in this respect, who attended strictly
to the *formal* structures of moral action. An ethic that
prematurely tries to give content to formal imperatives,
in abstraction from the concrete encounter in the moment,
is regarded by Bultmann as a highly dubious and prodi-
gious philosophical project. Philosophical ethics would do
better to confine itself strictly to a critical analysis of the
formal moral situation of man, the form of the command,
and the form of obedience, as did Kant, rather than
spuriously try to give situational content to the command.[39]

Bultmann's ethical formalism, which depends for content only upon the moment, differs from the formalism of
late Judaic legalism, which casuistically gave abstract
content to the command of God in the plethora of rules.
His formalism also differs from Kant's in his basic conviction that authentic moral knowledge is open to the
philosopher only as a possibility in principle, but is actualized as a possibility in fact only under the address of the
Christian proclamation.[40]

Having clarified Bultmann's crucial distinction between
ontological and ontic possibilities as well as the notion of
perverted intentionality, we now turn more specifically
to his view of natural moral knowledge.

B. The Limits of Natural Moral Knowledge

1. Pursuing an existential analysis of the ontology of man as such, we are especially concerned in this section to identify the limits and extent of his moral knowledge. Our sources for this complex discussion include many scattered passages in Bultmann's *Theology of the New Testament* as well as a number of essays, in particular "The Question of Natural Revelation," "The Crisis in Belief," "The Problem of Hermeneutics,"[41] "The Concept of Revelation in the New Testament,"[42] "Das Problem der 'Natürlichen Theologie,'"[43] and his lectures on "Jesus Christ and Mythology," as well as his programmatic essay on "The New Testament and Mythology."

Let us carefully frame the question at hand in this way: *Does man as such possess any kind of natural knowledge of God's demand?* Is the moral demand written into the ontology of man, i.e., from *within,* or does it encounter man as something from *without?* Kant's answer to this question is clear, viz., that man bears within the structure of his being as a man the rational capacity to perceive the moral law.[44] The answer of the Biblical witness is equally clear that the demand of God stands wholly *over against* and in no sense *within* the ontological structure of man.[45] Now we put the same question to Bultmann.

2. Bultmann first insists that knowledge of *God* and knowledge of *self* are inseparable. Man in his very search for authentic life has a preconscious relation to God. Frequently Bultmann quotes the classical statement of Augustine, "Thou hast made us for thyself, and our hearts are restless, until they rest in thee,"[46] as a witness to man's preconscious relation to God even in his searching for

authenticity. Is it thus incorrect to say that man has no
knowledge of God's demand prior to faith?

Man has a relation to God precisely amid his search
for self-fulfillment, whether conscious or unconscious. His
being is always moved by the search for God, however
unconsciously, since it is always moved by the question
of his own personal existence. *"The question of God and
the question of myself are identical,"*[47] Bultmann says.
Note that he does not say merely that these two questions
are inseparable or indistinguishable. They are identical.
When one knows himself properly, he knows of God;
when he asks concerning the ontology of man, he asks
already about God. This presupposition is determinative
for Bultmann's ethics.

Barth's assertion that the subject about which the Scrip-
tures speak is God of whom there can be absolutely no
prior understanding, is categorically rejected by Bultmann. "An *existentiell* knowledge about God is alive in
the form of the inquiry about 'happiness,' 'salvation,' the
meaning of the world and of history, and in the inquiry
into the real nature of each person's particular 'being.' "[48]

3. Bultmann uses the notion of *general revelation* to
denote this existential preknowledge of God that belongs
to man as such. In his essay "The Concept of Revelation
in the New Testament," he distinguishes between general
revelation and revelation in the New Testament. Revelation means the disclosure of what is concealed or the
opening up of what is hidden.[49]

Constantly confronted with limitations, man is forever
seeking to break through the boundaries that finite life
places upon him. Every man, consciously or unconsciously,
knows himself to be under limitation. *General revelation
is the opening up, in one or another of its many forms, of*

that which enables man to break through the boundaries that cut him off from the goals which to him represent authenticity.[50] Such an understanding of revelation belongs to every man in his knowledge of self-limitation. To know about revelation, in this sense, is to know about oneself. Such self-knowledge exists wherever men exist.[51]

Revelation in the New Testament differs from revelation in general in that it speaks of an event that stands in judgment upon all past modes of self-understanding, calling man to understand himself anew in terms of God's future.[52] We will deal with this later. Our present concern is to pursue the question of whether men have natural knowledge of God's demand. The crucial point concerning "general revelation" is that it is self-knowledge.

4. Although the object of Christian faith is the transcendent God, Bultmann surprisingly admits that "God in the Christian sense is nothing other than what he is for any other belief in which the idea of God is taken with all seriousness."[53] This statement is most confusing if taken alongside his later assertion that Christian knowledge of God is much more than man's knowledge of self-limitation.

What, then, do men mean by "God" insofar as that concept is subject to strict existential analysis? "God is he who bounds men,"[54] or he who constitutes the *limits* of human existence, Bultmann declares. Men everywhere know themselves as beings under limitations. They seek things they cannot attain; they are anxious for the morrow because they cannot secure their futures; they have a longing for what is true and beautiful and just, but these are not attainable. *God is knowable by* Daseins *analysis as that power which stands at the terminus of human striving, knowing, caring, longing, and obligation.*[55]

Why call this enigmatic power that hedges us in, "God"? Why not simply "the Unknown" or "fate"? Does not the name "God" gloss over the fact that man is at the mercy of an unfriendly, unknowable mystery?[56] The strange thing about Christian faith is that it has come to regard this mysterious power, not merely as a nameless fate, but as "my God," one who has met me as Redeemer.[57] Christian faith acknowledges this perplexing limiter as Savior. Such faith may be described as obedience insofar as it consists in giving up one's own claim upon this enigmatic power, acknowledging it as finally trustable and trustworthy. Christian faith knows that the meaning of life has its locus precisely in limitation and in the One who stands at the limit of human knowing.[58] But even existential analysis without benefit of the kerygma can know God as limiter.

5. Wherever men speak of God, they characteristically speak of him as one who makes *demands,* who places them under requirement. Included in the general knowledge shared by all men who speak of God, Bultmann suggests, is the idea that to God belongs holiness and omnipotence. Therefore when men know themselves to be under obligation, naturally they regard the transcendent God as the giver of the obligation.

Furthermore, whenever God's demands are spoken of, whether within or without the Christian community, they are regarded as something *beyond* the mere existence of the phenomenal world.[59] The term "God" is everywhere used to refer to that being which is *not* synonymous with the world or oneself. Even the ethics of autonomy contains a certain kind of transcendence, viz., the universal law of reason over against the subjective strivings of the appetitive will.[60]

But the fact that men speak of God and his demands does not necessarily mean they know God and truly understand the nature of his demand. Here is the surprising turn in Bultmann's argument: *the natural knowledge men have of God and his demands is "none other than man's knowledge of himself."*[61] Although men speak of the transcendent nature of the moral demand as *beyond* the human sphere and having its locus in God, what they *know* is merely self-knowledge of the human limitation situation. This point appears regularly whenever Bultmann discusses the possibility of natural theology.[62]

At this point we may begin to perceive a strange contradiction running through Bultmann's ethical analysis. On the one hand he has said that an existential knowledge of God is present in man's search for happiness and meaning. On the other hand he has said that general revelation or natural knowledge of God is self-knowledge. To state the ambiguity in another way: *man as such has knowledge of God, whether consciously or unconsciously, in his knowledge of himself as a being under limitation and requirement, but the object of his knowledge is not God but himself.*

Bultmann tries to sustain these contradictories with his presupposition that "the question of God and the question of myself are identical."[63] He fails to do so satisfactorily, however, unless he wishes to maintain that God and man are identical, which he does not. He merely wishes to say that when one raises the question about himself properly, he raises the question of the relation of himself to God. In the last analysis the object of man's self-knowledge must be either God or himself, since God and man are not synonymous, though they must always be related. Bultmann only confuses the issue by alternately suggesting that the object of self-knowledge is God, and yet it is not God.[64]

6. Let us further pursue Bultmann's twofold assertion that (*a*) the object of man's self-knowledge is not God and (*b*) that such self-knowledge leads to an impasse which only the revelation of God can illumine.

When men speak of an "omnipotent God" apart from the Christian *kērygma,* they are actually telling about their own human limitations, powerlessness, and constant subjection to forces from without.[65] Likewise when men talk of obedience to God apart from the self-understanding that proceeds out of the Christian proclamation, the source of their obedience is not another will but themselves. Man knows that he *is* not what he *ought* to be. Every man has such knowledge. He knows that in his actual (ontic, *existenziell*) situation he is never the self he ought to be. Even when he thinks he has fulfilled the law he constantly stands under fresh requirements.[66]

Such moral self-knowledge is not given only in the Christian proclamation, but is given to man as such and is subject to phenomenological analysis. Man knows that his life consists in a struggle to become an authentic self, i.e., really to be himself, to be what he *ought* to be. Yet at the same time man knows that he is always searching for this authentic self. At best he is "on the way" toward authentic self-fulfillment.[67]

It is with this kind of self-knowledge that man comes to speak prematurely of "God" and "God's demand." For it is plausible to natural man to assume that this moral self-knowledge is knowledge about God who presumably stands transcendently over against him. *It is natural for him to infer that in being obedient to this inner moral demand that is written into his ontological situation (to be who he ought to be) he is thereby being obedient to God.*[68]

Again Bultmann insists, however, that *"the knowledge contained in such talk about God is man's knowledge about himself."*[69] That which man actually obeys in such a context is not God, but merely man's conceptualization of that which limits, subjects, and confines him. Thus it is out of the human situation of imperfect action, unfulfilled intentions, guilt for the past, dread of the future, and existential knowledge that man *is* not what he *ought* to be that there comes talk about a transcendent demand divinely impinging upon man from without.[70]

Let us remember that Bultmann has earlier asserted most unequivocally that every man has a certain kind of knowledge of *God* in his existential self-knowledge, since "the question of God and the question of myself are identical." Now suggesting that such self-knowledge is not in the full sense knowledge of God, he thereby drastically qualifies his presupposition that self-knowledge and knowledge of God are identical.

We begin this section by asking whether man as such possesses any kind of natural knowledge of God's demands. Does the moral demand reside *within* man (autonomy) or encounter man as God's address (theonomy). Doubtless by now we perceive the difficulty of Bultmann's answer, which hinges on the identity of self-knowledge and knowledge of God. *On the one hand, Bultmann sees in the ontology of man a tension between is and ought that constitutes a preunderstanding of God's demand, but on the other hand, he hesitates to call this self-knowledge, knowledge of God.*

However, this uneasy position might more accurately be characterized as paradoxical rather than self-contra-

dictory.[71] For man always exists in the paradoxical state
of tension between his ontological possibilities and his
ontic possibilities, as outlined earlier in this chapter. As
the ontology of man may be existentially analyzed by adequate philosophy, it may be seen that every man knows
himself to be under requirement: to *be* who he *ought* to
be, to become an authentic self. The theologian sees the
demand of God as none other than authentic selfhood.
Thus man as such has a certain kind of knowledge of God
in that he knows himself to be under this requirement.
But in his *ontic* situation, he has always already lost the
possibility of becoming who he ought to be. The ontic
possibility for authentic life is given only in the address
of the Christian proclamation.

C. CONSCIENCE

1. The original meaning of conscience (*syneidēsis*),
according to Bultmann, was "a joint knowledge with
another," but by the time of Paul it had come to mean
"a knowledge shared with oneself."[72] It is that phase of
self-consciousness which scrutinizes and judges the intent
of one's mind (*nous*). It belongs to the ontological structure of man as such.

Bultmann regards conscience as *a universal human phenomenon.* Since every man has a relationship with himself, every man shares with himself knowledge of the
adequacy or inadequacy of his conduct in relation to the
requirements under which he stands.[73]

The judging conscience may either accuse or acquit
the self in its intentions and actions. The self may struggle
against the conscience. But though the self may even
subdue the conscience for a time, it never ceases to function as a judge demanding appropriate action from the

self. In every situation, conscience demands of man a specific attitude.[74]

2. The existential process to which the idea of conscience refers is essentially as follows. Man's life is a constant choosing toward possibilities in which the authentic self may be won or lost. It belongs to the ontology of man to strive to achieve authentic life, to fulfill himself in his choices, to seek goals that he understands as appropriate to his self-fulfillment.

For man to feel himself under obligation simply means that the goal toward which he strives has taken on the character of requirement or law.[75] Since human existence is a constant movement toward goals, it follows that every man knows himself constantly to be under requirement.

The idea of conscience therefore refers to this kind of moral self-knowledge which belongs to every man. When man fails to achieve the purposes that for him represent authentic life, conscience censures him. For every man lives constantly with the fundamental intention (*Grundintention*) of authentic life, though in actuality he is always missing this fundamental intention.[76]

We may recall that in *Jesus,* and in the essay on "The Understanding of Man and the World in the New Testament and the Greek World," Bultmann rejects all teleological thinking, since in it he sees the controlling presupposition that man is essentially in control of his future. He emphatically rejects the notion of man as being endowed with a predetermined *telos,* who by the habitual training of his will nurtures excellent actions that help him actualize his unique human purpose. Surprisingly, in his doctrine of conscience he now renovates teleological ethics and subordinates the entire idea of obligation to man's *telos.*

3. Is the self-knowledge contained in conscience therefore, properly speaking, a knowledge of God's demand?
Bultmann admits that, as Paul uses the term, the transcendent authority whose demand is known universally
through conscience is known by the Christian community
as God. It is for this reason that *pistis* and *hupakoē* may be
interchangeable terms for Paul.[77] Insofar as faith is obedience to God, Paul regarded it as an act of conscience. It
is in this sense that conscience becomes the highest court
of appeal in the ethics of Paul. Any man whose conscience
acquits him is no longer subject to any human authority.[78]
The verdict of conscience had ultimate validity for Paul
even if *in error* as to the content (*das Was*) of the requirement.[79]

The decisive feature of the conscience, according to
Bultmann's exegesis of Paul, is *that* it knows that there *is*
such a thing as "requirement" at all. It is not the specific
content (the "what") of its demand which makes it important but *that* it places man under a transcendent requirement. The Corinthians supposed themselves to be
obligated not to eat food offered to idols. Paul thinks their
conscience is "weak," and that they lack correct knowledge, but nevertheless the verdict of their conscience is
regarded by him as valid. They are bound by the verdict
of their conscience and should not be forced into conduct
that their conscience condemns.

Contrary to his previously expressed view that general
revelation is merely self-knowledge, Bultmann now argues that "the demand which conscience apprehends is
grounded in *a transcendent sphere over against man*."[80]
*Conscience is indeed man's self-knowledge, borne about
in the human self, belonging to the ontological structure
of man as such, but at the same time it remains that dis-*

tinctive feature of man's self-consciousness which witnesses to a transcendent authority beyond himself.[81] It is a metonomous witness within man as such.[82]

4. Bultmann's notion of conscience may be recognized as similar to Kant's view of autonomy. For autonomy is precisely this: the self has the moral law within itself. Rational man is a law unto himself. The key feature of autonomy is that the self bears within it, as a part of its ontological structure, the resident capacity to know the transcendent moral demand. Paul's notion of conscience represents for Bultmann precisely this resident capacity.

In order to make Bultmann consistent with himself, however, we must again return to his determinative distinction between ontological and ontic possibilties. Unfortunately he fails to make this distinction altogether clear in his interpretation of conscience, except in his brilliant exegesis of Rom., ch. 7. If this distinction is to be taken seriously, then we must conclude that *the knowledge given in conscience provides the ontology of man with an ever-present "possibility in principle" of knowledge of God's demand, but in view of man's ontic situation prior to faith (of guilt, dread, and superbia) he has always already lost this possibility.*

D. An Ambiguity in Greek Ethics

1. Bultmann is a historian. It is of considerable interest and not without relevance to our inquiry that we note his interpretation of certain classical patterns of ethical reflection. He often uses the ancient conflict between the Greek tragedians and the Sophists as an example of ethical types.[83] In this section, which is something of an excursus, we will outline Bultmann's interpretation of the transition in Greek ethics from the notion of the transcendent law

of the *polis* to its deterioration in the Sophists. This conflict is caught up in two great literary figures, Antigone and Creon.

The Greek world answered the question of anxiety by developing the *polis* (city-state) with its *nomoi* (laws).[84] Here man could find his real humanity, by being bound through the law to the *polis*. Human dignity and worth belonged to the man who existed in this ordered community. Freedom was perceived only in the context of this structure of law. But *does the law have a transcendent origin, or is it merely a product of human convention?* This is the urgent question that confronted the Greeks at the time of the tragedians. It is the fundamental question with which Greek ethics wrestles, Bultmann thinks, and finally the cause of its stumbling.[85]

In the earlier era of Greek ethics prior to the Sophists it was assumed that the *nomos* was divinely revealed from a source entirely transcending the wills of men. Greek mythology even to Plato tells of the gods bestowing the divine law upon the *polis*. It was in this way that the Greeks understood themselves as bound up in the divine order of the world. They understood that this order confronted them *in concreto* in the *polis*.[86] Plato tells, in the form of a myth, how Zeus sent Hermes to men to give them both *aidōs* and *dikē* (reverence and law). Only by being bound to the law in reverence was the Greek citizen able to achieve his freedom (*eleutheria*).[87]

Freedom for the ancient Greek, as for Kant, did not mean that man could do as he pleased. It was a freedom to serve the ordered rational community. The individual derived his dignity, not from himself per se, but from the fact that he stood in a responsible relation to the community of law.

The Greek citizen (again like Kant's autonomy) understood the law both as transcendent in its source *and* as the communal will of the citizens perceived by reason. The laws of the empirical community were regarded as harmonious with the divinely revealed law. It was from this special perspective that the ancient Greek felt that the divine law was self-legislated.[88]

Unfortunately, however, this ambiguity eventually caused the collapse of the *polis*. "For if on the one hand the *polis* and its *nomos* count as divine, and on the other hand they are actually made up of men, and are formed and governed in a concrete situation, then the idea of divinity is in danger of losing the sense of being a transcendent power beyond men's control."[89] Thus the idea of the transcendence of the law lost its authority when doubt arose in men's minds whether there was anything behind the moral demand of the community other than "the democratic assembly of the people who can annul and introduce *nomoi* at their pleasure."[90]

2. The Greek tragedians were preeminently concerned with this problem, warning that the human community would fall to pieces if it is not bound together by a transcendent order of authority. Sophocles' *Antigone* is the outstanding example Bultmann uses to set forth this conflict.[91] Curiously enough, some of Bultmann's most fascinating ethical analysis lies in his interpretation of Greek drama and poetry, quite apart from his Biblical exegesis. The chief characters in *Antigone*, Antigone and Creon, are viewed as ethical prototypes. Antigone personifies *radical reverence for the transcendent divine law, whereas Creon is one who makes his own will king.*[92]

Antigone is compelled to act against Creon, who had ordered her to ignore the divine law of Hades. Both appeal to Zeus and Dike to justify their actions. Antigone is put in the difficult position of maintaining that the true *nomos* is not a definable human statute, whereas Creon enjoys the advantageous position of being able to appeal to a positive, humanly legislated law that was clear and unambiguous. The transcendent law of Hades signified to Antigone that the *polis* was limited by a power over against it, viz., death, and that from the viewpoint of this transcendent power all human self-legislation was to be given a relative status.[93] This was essentially the viewpoint of the tragedians. Creon, on the other hand, "who does not acknowledge the transcendent basis of his office as sovereign, and therefore its limitations, but regards it as divine in its own right, becomes a tyrant in spite of his excellent maxims."[94]

Using this analogy from Greek literature, Bultmann argues that when man no longer understands himself as hemmed in by a transcendent moral demand, he sets himself up as an arbitrary self-legislative lawgiver.[95] Hesiod, Herodotus, Aeschylus, Sophocles, Pindar, and Plato all illustrate this thesis. "Sophocles shows in the *Antigone* how the law of the *polis* can only be genuine and valid when it is not a human ordinance, but when it is, on the contrary, founded on the 'unwritten, immutable laws of the gods.' "[96] The very essence of Greek tragedy, "the *hubris* in which man crosses the bounds of his humanity and thereby challenges the gods,"[97] remains yet as the theme of man's moral predicament.

3. Following Creon, it remained only for the Sophists to reduce the concept of *nomos* to the idea of thesis (*thesei*) and to inaugurate a new philosophical era from the presupposition that all moral demands arise out of mere human convention. *The Sophists overthrew the whole ancient Greek tradition of law, and in fact went to*

*the opposite extreme by regarding the law not as the re-
quirement of a transcendent authority, but as "the right
which everyone has against the other."*[98] This led to a
complete relativization of moral law.

Such was the crisis of the Greek *polis*. Bultmann regards
it as analogous to the crisis in contemporary morality.
"Greek religion did not have the strength to hold man
within the bounds of humanity."[99] After the crisis and
fall of the *polis*, the Greek understood his obligation to
law quite differently. The *nomos* was no longer regarded
as deriving its sanction from the gods, nor even from
nature (*phusis*), but it becomes reduced to mere *thesis*
which arises out of the consensus of individuals.[100] It rests
on contract and at times is even considered an imposition
on nature, an offense to man's humanity, hardly a product
of reason. The dictum of Protagoras that "man is the
measure of all things" sounded the keynote of the Sophist
revolt. After the collapse of the *polis*, Bultmann suggests,
man himself became the measurer of those requirements
for which obedience is due.[101]

The tragedians were concerned to dramatize the human
rebellion against the divine law and how man's pride
(*hubris*) in transgressing the measure appointed for him
evokes the nemesis of the gods.[102] But the skepticism and
this-worldliness that gained philosophical attire in the
Sophists succeeded in working a complete deterioration
of the transcendent basis for the law of the *polis*.

Thus in the figures of Antigone and Creon, Bultmann
sees the conflict between the tragedians and the Sophists
personified. Creon represents the aberration and deterioration of autonomy into irresponsibility and self-will. Antigone represents the ethics of the transcendent law on the
defense, under the attack of skeptical relativism.

E. The Paradox of Stoic Obedience

1. Bultmann draws a sharp contrast between the Christian view of obedience to the Word of God and the Stoic understanding of obedience to the eternal *logos*. This distinction will further clarify the differences between Bultmann and all autonomous ethics (especially Kant, who often reflects the Stoic pattern).

Stoic obedience consisted in subjecting oneself to the law of the *cosmos*, which was regarded as identical with the law of the inmost being of the rational man.[103] Stoic ethics presupposed a view of the world in which all things were pervaded by the divine *logos*. The rational self found security in the world by participating in the rationality of the *cosmos*. Authentic selfhood meant giving assent to the *logos*.

Bultmann perceives a "curious inconsistency"[104] in the Stoic view of obedience. It lies in the double meaning of the Stoic view of law: on the one hand it meant a cosmic law beyond the self, and on the other hand it meant a rational norm within the self. Thus *the source of the moral imperative for the Stoic was both within the self and written into the universe*. The same view of law is found in Kant, and most of the same problems.

2. The Stoic wise man conceived of obedience as the constant affirmation that everything that occurs does so through the causation of the universal *logos*. Emotion (*pathos*) is nothing but the vain effort of man to go against this universal causation. The *logos* lays its demands upon the human self for assent. The "curious inconsistency" that Bultmann finds in Stoic obedience is that *the cosmic* logos *does not work within human reason with the same inevitability that it seems to work in the order of*

natural occurrences. Yet obedience consists in the perfect correspondence of the rational self to the *logos.*[105]

Christian ethics categorically denies the rationalistic optimism that underlies Stoic obedience wherein the natural man is regarded as actually capable of the moral good.[106] The Christian understanding of life can agree with the Stoic in the assertion that when a man does evil he is not really doing what he *wants* to do, Bultmann says, i.e., he is going against the *Grundintention* of his striving, which is for authentic life. But the Stoic attributes disobedience to *error,* rather than to pride, guilt, or anxiety. The Stoic regarded disobedience as nothing other than reason pointing the will in a mistaken direction. Since reason is assumed to be capable of correction of the will, all that is needed for moral action is right reasoning. Christian ethics views man's wrongdoing, not as a mistake or rational error, but in the more profound sense that man is "radically incapable of doing what he wants to do"[107] because his will is under bondage to sin. It is useless to appeal to reason by telling a man he ought to do his duty. Thus the principle of autonomy, which for the Stoic (as for Kant) meant freedom and security in the world, thrusts the Christian into "the threshold of the abyss—the abyss of absolute moral subjectivity. . . . This subjectivity is required to give an account of itself, and incurs guilt."[108]

Stoic cosmology and ethics gave man a sense of security in an ordered world in which the order is internalized. Radical obedience, as it is understood in the Christian proclamation, in contrast undercuts all modes of reliance that are centered in this world. In the Stoic world view the whole of reality formed a unity that was permeated with a rational and divine power immanent within it.

It is in terms of this order that the Stoic found security through obedience. The reason that is internalized within man is merely an instance of the general rule that pervades all reality. In the Stoic world view "man sees himself as a particular instance of the general rule."[109] The ethics of radical obedience rejects this anthropology.

Obedience for the Stoic thus meant essentially that man is called to order his life as a unity just as the cosmos is an ordered unity, that he should strive for consistency as the universe is consistent, and that he must understand his purpose in life in the context of this universal purpose attested to in nature. When emotion stands in the way of this rational ordering, man cannot really be himself.[110]

3. Thus the Stoic thought that his obedience was a means to a kind of *freedom*, Bultmann says, which consisted in becoming lord over one's own inner self. Genuine freedom is achieved, not by seeking to control the environment or to change the rational order outside the self, but rather by looking within, to one's inner self, and seeking independence from the impingements of the outside world. The paradox that Bultmann discovers in Stoic ethics, which is of more significance than a mere historical curiosity, is that it is precisely in conformity to the rational order that the self finds release from dependence upon it.[111]

Only that which lies within the inner life (will, emotion, and imagination) was thought to be within man's power. To be able to recognize what is within one's power is a rational capacity residing in every man. No man is called to do anything except that which is within his power.

Thus Stoic ethics had both an outward direction (a movement away from the self) and an inward direction (a movement toward the self), according to Bultmann. On the one hand it sought conformity to the universal law of nature, and on the other hand self-control and the constraint of the emotions.[112] Stated differently, *rational obedience calls the self to absolute dependence upon the reasonableness of the order of nature, yet at the same time toward the radical independence of the self from external compulsions.*

The "detachment" that characterizes Stoic ethics follows from all this. The Stoic wise man thought he had nothing in the world to lose, since all things of ultimate import were within his subject self. He accepted suffering and regarded all earthly goods as *adiaphora.*[113] This detachment is not wholly unlike the detachment that characterizes eschatological existence in the Christian proclamation, according to Bultmann, in which a man does not place ultimate meaning in anything this side of the coming age. The difference, however, lies in the concept of the neighbor. Bultmann criticizes Stoic ethics as "individualistic," "negative," and "an ethics of withdrawal." He regards Stoic obedience as a turning away from the world, whereas Christian obedience calls men out of the world, only paradoxically to call them back into the world again.[114]

Recapitulation

We began our study of Bultmann with an analysis of radical obedience, showing how an existential view of man and an eschatological view of history became amalgamated in a unique view of Christian ethics. The central idea of this ethics is that man understands the concrete demand of the moment as God's demand, and that he is called to answer this demand with his total being and doing. The form that the demand of the moment always takes is love of the neighbor, but the content of the demand cannot be answered prior to or in abstraction from the situation.

We continued our study with an inquiry into Bultmann's analysis of the ontological structure of man as such, seeking to identify the extent and limit of man's natural moral knowledge. The principal findings of this chapter have been the determinative distinction between ontological and ontic possibilities, the identification of the central presupposition of Bultmann's ethical analysis that knowledge of God and self-knowledge are inseparable, and a review of some of the problems and ambiguities that arise out of the above distinction and the above presupposition. In the two excursuses above (on issues in Greek and Stoic ethics) we have examined certain typical historical patterns used by Bultmann as prototypes of ethical thinking.

Throughout this chapter on existential analysis, we have argued that an appropriate philosophical analysis can explicate the formal possibility of man for authentic life, but in Bultmann's judgment it cannot provide the actual self in its existential situation an ontic possibility of authentic existence. We have seen that Bultmann equivocates at the point of saying that self-knowledge and knowledge of God are identical. *However clearly he may say that natural knowledge of God is self-knowledge, and that proper self-knowledge is knowledge of God, he remains unwilling to admit indiscriminately that all self-knowledge is knowledge of God.* For although existential analysis of the ontology of man can hold before man the ontological possibility of authentic self-relatedness, Bultmann repeatedly has said that in man's *ontic* situation he has always already *lost* this possibility.

III

THE CHRISTIAN PROCLAMATION AS THE
TRANSFORMATION OF ETHICS

W<small>E WILL TAKE UP</small> exactly at the point of failure of existential analysis (*Daseinsanalyse*): the ontic situation of man as having always already lost the possibility of authentic selfhood. What we have dealt with in the preceding chapter is wholly amenable to an appropriate philosophical analysis. But again and again we have been confronted with the failure of such analysis to provide the existing individual in his concrete situation with an actual possibility of authentic life. Does Christian ethics merely reiterate this philosophical analysis of man, or does it provide the human situation with a distinctly new moral possibility?

This, then, is the decisive thing which distinguishes the New Testament from philosophy and the Christian faith from a "natural" understanding of existence: the New Testament speaks about and the Christian faith knows about a *deed of God which first makes possible man's self-surrender* (*Hingabe*), *his faith, his love—in short, his authentic life.*[1]

In this chapter we will inquire into the Christian proclamation of the deed of God that first makes possible authentic obedience, according to Bultmann, and ask how it constitutes a transformation of man's moral self-understanding. Precisely how does the Christian proclamation address man in his ontic situation with an actual "possibility in fact" of authentic obedience?

A. THE ACTUAL POSSIBILITY OF RADICAL OBEDIENCE

1. From what has been said concerning the ontology of man, it might appear possible to have a Christian understanding of existence without Christ, "as though what we had in the New Testament was the initial discovery and more or less clear expression—veiled in the garments of mythology—of an understanding of existence that is at bottom man's natural self-understanding, as it has been given clear expression in existentialist philosophy."[2] Heidegger's *Daseinsanalyse*, e.g., might appear to be no more than a profane philosophical presentation of the New Testament view of human existence.[3]

One might ask also how man can become obedient to God at all if obedience is a gift of God and not a self-willed effort, and how it can be required if it is outside the limit of human capacity?[4] Is obedience to God, according to the Christian proclamation, an original possibility with man, consonant with his natural disposition?

Bultmann's answer, as one might already suspect, is "yes and no"![5] *Yes*, insofar as Christian existence is the disposition of "genuine humanity," i.e., the life for which man was originally created. Faith, obedience, and love are not mysterious supernatural qualities, but the "natural disposition" of man, if one understands man in the sense of the "new creation" of the New Testament witness. "Natural" in this context does not mean "what is already given," but "what is appropriate to man's true nature."

Bultmann answers *no*, however, insofar as authentic existence cannot be achieved by a mere act of reflection on the part of natural man. This is precisely where the New Testament parts company with any philosophy which thinks that man can redeem himself. The existentialist philosophers may describe properly the ontology of man, but seldom do they take seriously enough the radically fallen condition of actual human existence.[6]

Philosophy is convinced that all we need is to be *told* about man's "nature" in order to realize it. Bultmann does not regard such self-confidence as justified. In any event the New Testament is clear in affirming the total incapacity of man to free himself from his factual fallenness, and that deliverance can only come by an act of God.[7]

Although the New Testament hardly provides us with an existential analysis of the nature of man, it does proclaim an event of redemption that addresses man in his ontic situation with a new and actual possibility of truly human existence.[8] *Since it understands that man's new moral possibility is given in an event, the saving act of God, it also understands that without this event man's situation is one of despair, an assertion that philosophy rejects.* How can the New Testament maintain this, in contrast to the whole weight of the philosophical tradition?

2. Both the New Testament and philosophy of existence agree that man can always be and become only what he already is.[9] As the idealist calls man to "Become what you are," so Heidegger summons man to *Entschlossenheit* (decisiveness), which is what he already is. Similarly, the New Testament exhorts Christians to be holy because they have already been made holy (I Cor. 6:11), to walk in the Spirit because they are already in the spirit (Gal. 5:25). All agree that authentic life is possible only on the basis of the fact that man by grace already stands in it. But the difference is that the New Testament speaks thus

only to those who believe, never to natural man. The New
Testament denies that man as such already possesses an
ontic possibility for authentic life.[10]

The New Testament knows that man can be and become only what he already is, and that man as such, apart
from Christ, does not stand in his true being, is not as he
ought to be, is not alive, but dead.[11] The existentialist
philosopher may think the self can be fully aware of its
fallenness, but the question the New Testament raises is,
*"How can man be aware of his fallenness if he himself is
completely fallen?"*[12] The philosopher is mistaken in thinking that all man needs is to be told that he is fallen. Man's
plight is more desperate.

Philosophical analysis constantly confuses man's ontological possibility with his ontic possibility, mistaking a
possibility in principle for a possibility in fact. It correctly
perceives the theoretical possibility of authentic self-
relatedness but prematurely regards it as an actual possibility. This error is based on the spurious confidence that
knowledge about man's true being makes man already the
master of it.[13] Even Heidegger regards man as such as
fully capable of achieving authentic life. Heidegger summons man to shoulder the accident of his destiny in the
face of nothingness, and to *decide* who he shall be. This
is analogous to "Religion A" in Kierkegaard's "stages," or
"the despair of willing despairingly to be oneself" in
Sickness Unto Death.

3. In view of this, the New Testament asserts that the
only reasonable attitude for man to adopt apart from
Christ is one of despair.[14] Of course, Bultmann admits, it
cannot prove its assertion, any more than the philosophers
can prove theirs. It is a matter for decision. In any event,
the New Testament addresses man as one who is always

already a self-assertive rebel who possesses no ontic possibility of obedience to God apart from the sheer gift of God. It tells man that his radical self-assertion[15] makes him blind to the fact of his own self-assertion, and this in itself is the clearest evidence of the fallenness of man. In his self-assertiveness, man closes himself against the possibility of understanding his life as self-surrender. It seems that it might be possible for man of himself to conquer this self-assertiveness, but Bultmann insists this is precisely the possibility against which he has closed himself in his self-assertiveness. *Being who he is, i.e., being self-assertive, man cannot escape the self-assertiveness that makes him think he can escape it.*[16]

Thus man is incapable of realizing the authentic life which he can formally know (as an ontological possibility) since however hard he tries, in everything he does he remains himself, self-assertive man. Therefore, true self-hood becomes an authentic possibility for man only when he is delivered from himself.

4. It is the claim of the New Testament that this is exactly what has taken place. Bultmann takes this to be precisely the meaning of the Christ occurrence.[17]

Eschatological existence has therefore become an actual possibility for man through the fact that *God has acted,* and the world as "this world" has come to an end, in that *man himself has been made new.*[18]

This is the meaning of the Pauline declaration that man is a "new creature," and the Johannine declaration that he is "born again."[19] *God's love encounters man as a power that embraces him and sustains him, even and precisely amid his fallenness and self-assertiveness.* God accepts man for what he is not, and this means that God frees him from himself as he is.[20]

The occurrence which takes place in Christ, therefore, is
the revelation of God's love which frees man from himself
and for himself by freeing him to a life of commitment in
faith and love. Faith, as man's freedom from himself, as openness for the future, is only possible as faith in God's love.
Faith in his love, however, is still self-assertion so long as this
love is only man's wishful thinking. It is an abstract idea so
long as God has not revealed his love. It is for this reason
that the Christian faith is a faith in Christ, i.e., because it is
faith in the revealed love of God. Only he who is already
loved can love. Only those who have received trust as a gift
can show trust in others. We are free to give ourselves to God
because he has committed himself to us.[21]

It is in this way that the Christ occurrence addresses man
with a viable possibility of radical obedience to God.

B. The New Point of Departure: The Christ Event

1. Consequently Christian ethics proceeds out of utterly different presuppositions than the ethics of natural-
ism or idealism. Obedience to the self-disclosing God
stands in radical contrast to all of man's natural self-
assertive efforts to know and do the good.

*Christian ethics has its uniqueness in that it speaks of
an event which gives it the right to speak of the demand
of God, and not merely man and his knowledge of himself.*[22] This event is Jesus Christ, in whom a special Word
is spoken to man by God. According to the New Testament witness, we may be assured that in this event we
encounter "God as one who stands over against us,"[23] not
merely our self-knowledge. Upon this event is based a
message which confronts man as God's Word, "not teaching him a new idea of God, but giving him the right to
believe in the God in whom he truly might believe."[24]

It is from this event that man comes to learn of the One

to whom he is ultimately responsible. Christian obedience finds its beginning point in "this one Word—found in the New Testament and based on the Christ event—which is God's Word."[25] The scandal of Christian belief is that God has made his Word known in an event, and in this particular event.

2. But what specifically can it mean to modern man to say that *God acts* in Christ? Bultmann makes no attempt to speak about God as he is "in himself."[26] To the contrary he insists with Melanchthon: *Christum cognoscere hoc est: beneficia eius cognoscere.*[27]

If modern man is to speak of God's action without mythology, he must do so without objectifying it into a worldly occurrence. Yet if talk of God's act is to be meaningful, it cannot be simply figurative or symbolic. "To speak of the act of God means at the same time to speak of my own existence."[28] Consequently Bultmann is forced to speak of God's action neither mythologically nor "symbolically," but analogically, in the sense that "we represent God's act as analogous to human action."[29]

Mythological thinking represents the divine action as something that breaks into natural, historical, and psychical life as a "miracle," an idea, which, in its ordinary form, Bultmann believes modern man incapable of taking seriously. Only insofar as the divine action is understood as taking place *in* rather than *between* worldly occurrences can the true unworldliness or other-sidedness of God's action be maintained. Even then, God's act is hidden from every eye except the eye of faith. The only thing generally visible is the "natural occurrence." It is precisely *within* this occurrence that God's action takes place.[30] *"The paradox of faith* is that it understands an event that is demonstrable in its natural and historical context as God's deed,"

says Bultmann. "The element of *nevertheless* is inseparable from faith."[31]

But is not God's action thereby drawn into the whirl-
pool of subjectivity if it can be spoken of only at the same
time human existence is spoken of? Bultmann answers that
it does not thereby follow that God is not real apart from
the believer or the act of belief. For human existence takes
place only in encounter with that which is different from
it.[32] In subjectivizing the divine action, we forget that
man is a historical being, not a being in isolation.[33]

We have been inquiring into the meaning of the proclamation that "God acts." The main point is that just as
the self-understanding which proceeds out of God's act
cannot be separated from God's act, so the alleged divine
act cannot be separated from the self-understanding that
proceeds out of it.[34]

3. If God's act can be spoken of only as I speak of
myself, have we thus eliminated the usual idea of an event
as a definite occurrence of the past? And have we not
denied that God has acted once for all for the whole world
in Christ, whether we respond to it or not?[35]

The answer can be given in a single sentence, that *God
encounters us in his Word*—namely, in a specific word, in
the proclamation which began with Jesus Christ. For one may
indeed say that God encounters us always and everywhere;
but we do not see and hear him everywhere—as Luther frequently said—unless his Word comes and adds itself and
through its light makes the particular moment understandable
for us.[36]

That the Christ event did occur as a discrete event of the
past is clearly affirmed by Bultmann, for only in this way
can the Word of God really be *verbum externum*. Never
is it *verbum externum*, however, as a possession that we

secure through knowledge, but only as an *address* that encounters us again and again.[37]

That God has acted in Jesus Christ is not, however, a demonstrable historical fact. "Jesus of Nazareth is not the Word of God for the objectifying view of the historian."[38]

As the Word of God, Christ is *ante me et extra me*—not, however, as something objectively demonstrable and chronologically datable *ante me,* but as the *Christus pro me* who encounters me in the Word. The eschatological occurrence which is Christ realizes itself always only *in concreto,* here and now, where the Word is preached (II Cor. 6:2; John 5:24) and evokes faith or unfaith (II Cor. 2:15 f.; John 3:18; 3:36).[39]

Consequently, the Word of God and the church belong together insofar as the church is constituted by the Word as the community of those who are obedient to the Word. But as the Word is God's Word only as event, so also the church is really church only as event.[40]

4. We have seen earlier that man as such may prematurely think he possesses knowledge of God's demand when the object of his knowledge is actually self-knowledge of his human situation of finitude and limitation.[41] Christian obedience differs from such self-knowledge in that it lives out of an event in which God himself is disclosed to man. On the basis of the new self-understanding that this event makes possible, Christian belief asserts that all inquiry about God's demand rooted in man's natural self-understanding is basically illusory, since it assumes that man can reach for knowledge of God, rather than receive it as a gift in the here and now.[42]

Equating the voice of conscience with the voice of God is equally disastrous. For although all men know they *are* not what they *ought* to be, this self-knowledge con-

stitutes merely a "pre-understanding"[43] of the demand of
God. It should not be inferred that this knowledge of conscience, resident in man's ontology, is, properly speaking,
authentic knowledge of God's demand.[44] *When the holiness of God is taken seriously, all talk of knowledge of
God as a possession of man in the faculty of conscience
must come to an end.* The Christian proclamation calls
man to acknowledge himself as sinner, "and his history as
a history of sinful men, and therefore . . . (the knowledge
of conscience) enshrouds God in a veil."[45] It is precisely
when man comes to this self-knowledge that he is a sinner, utterly empty of knowledge of God's will, that he
begins to look toward God instead of toward something
within himself for salvation and moral knowledge. Christian obedience has its beginning point exactly here, says
Bultmann, with the self-understanding that man can
finally do nothing good of himself, but that God has acted
to make what is good known to man.[46]

Man cannot infer the fullness of God in some transcendent
sphere from the absence of God in the here and now. All talk
of the transcendent God *becomes illusory when it is an attempt to be more than a mere negation,* that is, more than the
admission that the actual reality of man is devoid of God.[47]

Thus all inquiry about God, prior to Christian belief, if
taken seriously, puts man in the situation of being "on the
lookout" for God's presentation of himself in an event of
grace. This event of grace is precisely what the Christian
proclamation announces.[48]

In an essay entitled "Die liberale Theologie und die
jüngste theologische Bewegung" (1924), Bultmann asserts
that when the Word of God speaks to man it always means
"the total annulment of man, his negation, his being called
into question, and judgment upon all things human."[49]

This view is neither skepticism nor pessimism, he says, because both skepticism and pessimism take their criteria from man. In the New Testament we find the radical denial of all human claims, and the calling into question of all the values, criteria, and goods of man as such.[50]

Christian obedience does not arise out of these values, claims, and criteria, but only in response to the special deed of God on behalf of men. The scandal of Christian ethics, says Bultmann, is not that it requires a *sacrificium intellectus* which repudiates modern knowledge, but that it requires man to acknowledge his total dependence upon God for authentic life which involves the negation of all man's striving to achieve life by himself.[51]

5. Summarizing to this point, Bultmann has argued that (*a*) out of *natural man's* self-knowledge that "he *is* not what he *ought* to be," he easily *infers that his feeling of "oughtness" must have its source in a Demander beyond himself,* and thus he comes to speak of God as the ground of obligation; but (*b*) *the knowledge that men attain in this alleged divine Ought is none other than self-knowledge,* and that (*c*) *all talk of the transcendent God on the part of man as such becomes illusory when it is an attempt to be more than a mere negation,* or an admission that the actual situation of man is devoid of knowledge of God. This is the center of Bultmann's unique treatment of natural revelation. All man's alleged knowledge of God's demand is self-knowledge, and stands as *preparatio evangelica.* (*d*) *Christian obedience takes its distinctive beginning point from the proclamation of the deed of God that claims man with love, by accepting him even in his self-assertion in such a way that an authentic self-relation now becomes an ontic possibility for him.*

It is beyond the purview of this inquiry to ask in detail

about the nature of the Christ event. If we have sought in this section, however, to set forth Bultmann's view of the deed of God as the distinctive presupposition of the Christian understanding of obedience to God, and consequently to sharpen the distinction between natural moral knowledge and Christian moral knowledge, we now must clarify the relation between faith and obedience.

C. FAITH AND OBEDIENCE

1. Bultmann speaks of obedience as a part of the "structure" of faith. Faith is the attitude of man in which he receives the gift of the righteousness of God through which the divine deed of salvation becomes realized within man.[52] Faith is an act of obedience in which man surrenders all his "boasting," all desire to live on his own resources, all adherence to tangible realities, and assents to the scandalous fact of a crucified Lord.[53] Faith is both the requirement made and the gift offered in preaching. Since it is man's *answer* to the Word of God, it is always an act of obedience.[54]

In this act of obedience man is freed *for* his authentic self by being freed *from* himself (the phony self burdened by guilt which has been brought into the present).[55] Bultmann regards obedience as the most important subsidiary concept for the explication of the meaning of faith. *If faith requires total self-surrender, it must be obedience.*[56]

The Christian message carries with it a *demand*. This demand consists essentially in calling the hearer to surrender his previous understanding of himself.[57] It demands a total reversal of the previous direction of the will and intentionality of man. Paul terms this *hupakoē pisteōs*, the obedience of faith.

"Faith as obedience" stands in radical opposition to

boasting.[58] It must not be viewed as an accomplishment, which is an attitude in which the will still asserts itself. If obedience thinks it has a right to be proud of itself as an accomplishment of the will, then it has already ceased to be a *deed* and become a *work,* and thus is not radical obedience.

Bultmann finds it inadequate to conceive of the Christian understanding of faith *primarily* as trust, or as repentance, or as experience, or as disposition, or as virtue. In contrast to all these, he says, the New Testament regards faith primarily as obedience—a radical renunciation in which one surrenders one's prior self-understanding with its striving for self-righteousness and receives the message of God's righteousness. In one excursus Bultmann goes so far as to declare, *"pistis = hupakoē."*[59] Faith *is* that obedience in which the self renounces all that had been its pride and gain in its existence under the law.[60]

2. Such obedience is not a quality that adheres to man[61] as if the quality might remain with man apart from its dependent relation to God's deed. On the contrary, the obedience of faith cannot be abstracted out of relationality in such a way that it becomes man's possession. It is not a virtue.

Since obedience is not a quality, it has no temporal durability. If it has become a present possibility, "this 'present-ness' is not a temporal and as such a temporary state; rather, its 'present-ness' is that of the eschatological Now."[62] Obedience never exists in a past moment. Its continuity can never be ensured.

"Faith as obedience," Bultmann declares, means "being free and open for the future,"[63] since one leaves behind anxiety (*Sorge*) about himself and acknowledges that the future belongs to God. Such obedience constantly directs

man's attention away from himself and toward the suf-
ficiency of God, but always in such a way as to make
him conscious of his responsibility to his neighbor.[64]

3. Bultmann also speaks of obedience as risk or venture
(*Wagnis*). *In the obedience of faith, one ventures his
doing in faith and ventures his faith in doing.* Such obedience is not

a possession of my "inner life," on which I can look occasionally, and from which I would then have to direct my glance
again to the other side, to my "tasks and duties, necessities
and temptations."[65]

Rather, one is *only* obedient *ever anew in* his tasks and
duties. One does not *have* faith, and then put it to the
test, says Bultmann. One has faith only *as* he puts it to
the test, and *risks* it in obedience.[66]

Consequently the obedience of faith is described by
Bultmann as a movement between the "no longer" and
"not yet." In the moment of obedience the past takes on
the character of that which is overcome.[67] It is "no
longer." The message of forgiveness declares that the
past is, in effect, clothed with Christ's righteousness.

The "not yet" of obedience is that hope which surrenders all security and lives toward the future as God's gift.
In the moment of obedience one waivers all earthly
securities and all attempts to dispose of one's future. The
obedient man trusts in the "not yet" as that which is
finally secured by God. Since obedience is always a decision and must be recapitulated again and again in each
moment, it always is characterized by this special movement between "no longer" and "not yet."[68] Thus obedience
is constantly a venture.

4. When Bultmann speaks of faith as acceptance of the
Christian kerygma, he does not mean assent or agreement,

but "true obedience which includes a new self-understanding."[69] Such obedience cannot be an act that takes place once for all, nor can it be an "experience" to which one might look back as a past event, nor can it be a feeling that occasionally emerges, interrupting the ordinary course of feelings and experiences.[70] Rather, it must shape the whole of Christian existence in the manifold historical reality of the believing self. *There is no moment in which the man of faith regards himself as temporarily released from the obedience that faith requires.* Thus obedience "realizes itself in concrete living" in all of the individual acts of the man of faith.[71]

Bultmann protests the notion that righteousness implies ethical perfection. In the New Testament, righteousness is an eschatological verdict that God pronounces over man in the present. Hence it does not mean "sinlessness," but instead the divine verdict that the sinner's sins do not count against him. Bultmann seeks to preserve both the juridical meaning of righteousness as a forensic act of God, and at the same time the eschatological contemporaneousness (*Gegenwärtigkeit*) of righteousness. Further, the "right-wised" man is not merely "regarded as if" he were righteous, but rather he *is* from God's point of view pronounced righteous. This forensic-eschatological verdict bears an imperative for the hearer to "become who he is!" Thus righteousness is not an "ethical quality that resides in man," but rather God's verdict upon man in the present.[72]

5. To what extent is such obedience a kind of "knowledge" (*Wissen, gnōsis*)? The New Testament speaks of the self-understanding of the man of faith as a form of *gnōsis*, but *gnōsis* in this case refers not merely to perception of an object but to the participation of the knower

in that which is known, and consequently a new existential self-understanding. Insofar as this self-understanding unfolds objective knowledge (*Objekterkenntnis*) it does not fully explain itself.[73]

Since faith is always simultaneously confession, Bultmann admits that it always has an object, viz., God's saving deed in Christ. He insists that Christian obedience is not "obedience in general" but the obedience of faith in this particular message of God's deed as it meets man in the present. Opposing a pietistic conception of the obedience of faith as an obedience without any content of knowledge,[74] he asserts, somewhat surprisingly, that the obedience of faith has a *dogmatic* character insofar as it is related to the objective proclamation of the Christian community. It has an *undogmatic* character, however, insofar as it is clear that the Christian proclamation is no mere report of a past incident that could simply be regarded as "true" without the existential transformation of the hearer's own existence.[75]

Although obedience is not without an object, the object is not a "doctrine about the objective facts of the case,"[76] *but rather personal address.* This address is objective insofar as it meets the self from without the self. It is *kērygma*, which lays claim upon the hearer. Thus *hupakoē* always springs from *akoē*, the hearing of this particular word.[77]

6. Christian existence is a life of obedience. For Bultmann this means that man's total life comes under the determination of a renewed self-understanding that is an actual possibility because of the act of God. The life of the individual is no longer from and toward himself, but now lives from and toward the divine deed of salvation. *The Christ event becomes the "determinant of concrete life."*[78] This determination is not a general determination,

but a specific determination of one's actions, even, says Bultmann, "to the details."[79]

As such, the obedient life is an existence shaped by the spirit (*pneuma*).[80] The power of the obedient life, according to the New Testament, is the spirit. Even in the earliest preaching the spirit was regarded as the creator of the obedient heart.[81] The Hellenistic understanding of *pneuma* was that of a power which was more or less durably bestowed upon man. This stands in contrast to the *spontaneous* view of spirit found in the Old Testament, which characteristically was given in and for a *specific* situation and took possession of the whole man in a particular moment. The earliest church, according to Bultmann, made more use of the Hellenistic view, as a power which, when once given, gives the entire life a special character, imparting certain qualities that were not present before in the will.[82]

It is in this way that Bultmann employs the concept of radical obedience to clarify the New Testament understanding of faith. Faith and obedience are necessary correlates precisely because the Christian proclamation carries with it a demand for a new self-understanding.

IV

INDICATIVE AND IMPERATIVE

HAVING ESTABLISHED that authentic obedience to God
has become an ontic possibility for man only by
virtue of the act of God in which man himself has been
made new, and in which the love of God embraces man
even in his self-assertiveness in a way that he can now
love and trust others since he himself is loved and trusted,
we come now to ask how this indicative constitutes an
imperative. If man himself has been "born again" and
become a "new creature" through the act of God in the
Christ event, what must he do to become who he is, or
how is he called to act as a new creature?

A. THEIR PARADOXICAL JUXTAPOSITION

1. In the New Testament proclamation many statements seem to assume that the new creation is an accomplished fact. "The old man has passed away." "You are a
new creation." "The Son has set you free." These are
statements in the indicative mood. They simply indicate
a state of existence. On the other hand, we find in the
New Testament many statements in the imperative mood,
which seem to assume that Christian existence is *not* an
accomplished fact, but rather that it demands human
decision for its actualization. In this section we shall inquire into the way in which Bultmann relates these two

dimensions of the Christian proclamation, a dialectic that doubtless constitutes one of his most constructive contributions to ethics.

Bultmann's essential proposal is that indicative and imperative are not two things, but one. *The imperative is "hidden" within the indicative, and the indicative is "hidden" within the imperative.* They cannot be separated in such a way as to say that one implies the other, as a first implies a second. Rather, they belong together as two sides of a coin. This is the "internal unity" (*die innere Einheit*) of indicative and imperative.[1]

2. This relationship is captured in Paul's phrase, "If we live by the Spirit, let us also walk by the Spirit" (Gal. 5:25). It is here presupposed that the hearer understands himself as given the actual possibility of new life in the Spirit, through God's deed in Christ.[2] Yet, the indicative, that we live by the Spirit, must be explicitly realized, or laid hold of, by man's decision to *walk* by the Spirit. This is obedience: *to become who you are;* to obey the imperative that is concealed in the indicative.[3]

This does not mean *"Werde, wer du bist!"*[4] in the sense in which this was said in German idealism, i.e., approximating the perfect ideal of humanity. Bultmann strongly resists the notion of the Christian life as a striving toward an ideal condition, as if the Christ event might be regarded as an ideal type of humanity that men are called to try to achieve. Becoming who one is, however, is the heart of the ethics of the New Testament, insofar as the Christ event is understood as the forensic-eschatological deed of God in which man has been made new by virtue of God's saving deed and insofar as man is called to become the new creature which he already *is* according to God's verdict.[5]

3. Typically Bultmann regards the Johannine sources

as those providing the clearest formulation of the paradoxical relation of indicative and imperative. The essential formula is this: that *"out of the love we have received arises the obligation to love."*[6] Again and again in the Johannine writings this formula appears:

"We love, because he first loved us." (I John 4:19.)

"A new commandment I give to you, that you love one another; even as I have loved you, that you also love one another." (John 13:34.)

"Beloved, if God so loved us, we also ought to love one another." (I John 4:11.)

Bultmann points out that the Johannine imperatives, such as "Abide in my love,"[7] are regularly linked with indicative formulations, such as "If you keep my commandments, you will be abiding in my love."[8] Faith and love, or better, faith active in love,[9] form the same unity as the juxtaposition of the indicative and imperative. In faith it is decided "in advance" (*im voraus*) that all action is to be in love, although love can never be offered "in advance."[10]

4. Another way of expressing the paradoxical juxtaposition of indicative and imperative is in the formula "no longer" and "not yet," which we discussed earlier.[11] The paradox of eschatological obedience is that the redeemed man is no longer of this world, and yet his reconciled life as a new being is never so complete that it can be looked upon as an accomplished fact.

Consequently the faithful man is constantly "on the move" to become who he *is* in the light of the new age inaugurated in Christ, and consequently always between the "no longer" and the "not yet." In the salvation occurrence, an ontic possibility[12] has been given to man which he is called continually to decide to accept and make concrete in his own existence.[13] Obedience involves acceptance of this possibility.

But "we are what we are in hope,"[14] says Bultmann repeatedly. Obedience is never an accomplished fact, as if the self could look upon it as a past event and be proud of it. It is only in the mode of hope that man may presently exist as a completed new creation. Thus he stands continually under the imperative to *be* reborn. It is for this reason that the ethics of the New Testament not only declares to man that he *is* a new creature but calls upon him not to be conformed to his old life under subjection to alien powers. He must put off his old nature with its practices and its false self-understanding. *He is called to bring into actuality the new man, which the salvation occurrence has made possible and imperative.*[15]

Bultmann states the same paradoxical juxtaposition as it appears in Paul:

In this contradiction it becomes clear that he who is baptized belongs as such to the world to come. But in his present provisional situation of existence, he *is* not yet what he *ought* to be and what he *sub specie Dei* is. But, nevertheless, his belonging to the coming age determines his existence in the present.[16]

5. It is a matter of considerable interest to Bultmann that the church's understanding of the relation of indicative and imperative underwent a major transformation in the first two centuries, deteriorating constantly after Paul and John, with few exceptions. As a matter of fact, the way in which various writers understand the relation of indicative and imperative becomes for Bultmann one of the principal yardsticks for determining the importance of their message.

His general conclusion in Part Three of *Theology of the*

New Testament is that *in its second-century developments the church increasingly* viewed obedience as a meritorious work and not infrequently as a condition for attaining salvation.[17] It tended to lose the Pauline-Johannine insistence that obedience is the gift of grace, and freedom is the freedom to obey.[18] The imperative came again to have the character of a law, and almost entirely lost its paradoxical relation to the indicative. Moralistic piety replaced the eschatological consciousness that was present in the earliest community, and thus the basis for radical obedience was lost.[19]

Ignatius is a noted exception to this rule, and to some degree also the First Letter of Clement. *"Being,* therefore, a holy portion,"* says Clement, *"let us *do* all that belongs to sanctification."*[20] "Being who one is," or becoming by one's decisions the right-wised man of whom the eschatological proclamation speaks (the same dialectic found in the Pauline-Johannine traditions), is a theme that continues to reflect the most authentic core of New Testament ethics.

By the time of the pastoral epistles, however, the paradoxical tension had almost disappeared. The crucial exegetical use that Bultmann makes of this hermeneutical principle of the unity of indicative and imperative witnesses to its centrality in his theology as a whole.[21] In his exposition of the theology and ethics of the later New Testament tradition[22] he seems definitely to reject any conception of faith or obedience that does not measure up to the Pauline or Johannine standard. This provides substantial grounds for the assumption we have made that Bultmann's own view of Christian existence is the same as that which is explicated as Christian existence in Paul and John.

B. FREEDOM AND OBEDIENCE

1. Kant defines freedom as the determination of the will by the rational law. Thus it is synonymous with obedience. No one is more free, according to Kant, than the man who obeys the categorical demand of the moral law. In fact, Kant argues that we know man is free only because we know him to be under requirement.[23] It is with surprise and interest that we note an astonishingly similar dialectic of freedom and obedience in Bultmann.[24]

Obedience is the surrender of one's prior self-understanding in which he tried to live *for himself*, despairingly attempting to achieve authentic life by his own power. Obedience involves the total submission of the self to God's grace. In doing so, man finds release from those powers which held him in bondage in his former self-understanding. It is for this reason, Bultmann says, that *obedience to God may be described as freedom.*[25]

This freedom arises from the fact that the new man no longer understands that he belongs to himself, and thus no longer bears the anxiety for his own life, but instead lives in total subjection to God's grace.[26] This is the "freedom for which man is set free" by the salvation occurrence. It is the freedom to obey, and the obedience that constitutes freedom.[27]

Freedom, in the New Testament, is not a base of operations for the flesh (*sarx*). It is properly understood neither as a release from binding moral norms, nor from the law of God, but rather a new servitude.[28] It is an *enslavement* to righteousness, in contrast to man's former enslavement to sin. It is obedience to God, rather than obedience to *sarx*. The paradoxical witness of the New Testament, however, is that in becoming a "slave of

Christ" one becomes a "freedman of Christ." In such
obedience one is made free to serve the neighbor, and
such freedom understands itself under requirement to
meet the neighbor's need. Thus freedom is realized in
obedience, and obedience in freedom.[29]

2. An adequate philosophical analysis of man (*Daseins-analyse*) is able formally to set forth and describe the
essential relation of freedom and obedience, writes Bult-
mann, but it cannot concretely endow man with either
freedom or obedience.[30] It may urge man to take anxiety
upon himself and in freedom decide to be open to the
future, but, as we have said, it cannot provide man with
the actual possibility of freedom.[31] Such freedom can only
be *given* to man, and of course, this is precisely what the
gospel is concerned to declare. Since man *is forgiven* of
his sin, and met with God's love even in his pride and
self-assertiveness, he is enabled to be free, and thus to be
obedient.

It is freedom *from* ourselves as the old selves, and *for* ourselves as the new selves. It is freedom from the illusion,
grounded in sin, that we can establish our personal existence
through our own decision.[32]

In his Gifford Lectures, Bultmann contrasts the Renais-
sance-Enlightenment view that freedom is freedom *from*
authority, with the traditional Christian view that freedom
is always freedom *under* authority, and thus a freedom
that is known only in obedience.[33]

We may note that we are merely restating the relation
of indicative and imperative in this formulation of freedom and obedience. "The indicative gives expression to
the new self-understanding of the believer," Bultmann
writes, "for the statement 'I am free from sin' is not a
dogmatic one, but an existential one. It is the believer's

confession that his whole existence is renewed. . . . The imperative reminds him that he is free from sin, provided that his will is renewed in obedience."[34]

Only when the relation between freedom and obedience is understood, Bultmann declares, is the imperative of the New Testament properly conceived. His basic formulation of this relationship is: *"Freedom is the ground of the demand, and the demand actualizes freedom."*[35]

3. This twofold relation is expressed in *the proclamation of Jesus that calls men to be both radically free and radically responsible.* On the one hand, man is declared to be free from legalism, and from the scribe who would interpret for him the demands of the moment in minute detail. Man is free from this "heavy burden" which Pharisaic obedience puts upon him.[36] He is no longer under the necessity of constantly searching for the correct "general" mode of action, because all he needs to do is listen to the demands of the situation in order to know the demand of God.[37] There is no special "expert knowledge" of God's demands in the possession of the professional religionist. The tax collector, adulterer, and sinner are no farther from knowledge of God's demands than the scribe or lawyer.

On the other hand, however, Jesus' eschatological ethics makes man radically responsible. It allows and demands that he constantly regard himself as called to ultimate decision before God in every penultimate decision. It presents him with an eschatological either/or in every moment of encounter with the neighbor. Man is no longer in position to shift responsibility for interpretation of the demand of the moment to some "rule" or "principle."[38] He is responsible only amid his freedom and free only amid his responsibility.

C. GOSPEL AND LAW

1. In our pursuit of Bultmann's view of the relation of indicative and imperative, having reviewed the basic dialectic of freedom and obedience, we now turn to the analogous dialectic of gospel and law. Is the obedient man under the law? In what sense is Christ the end of the law? How does the law continue to meet the radically obedient man?

We will begin by suggesting that the term "law," as Bultmann understands its New Testament usage, is equivalent to the more general term "demand." *The law is understood as any requirement under which man understands himself, which proposes to show man what he ought to do in order to achieve authentic selfhood.* Thus in the New Testament, the law was conceived as "the totality of historically given requirements."[39] The Old Testament Torah, therefore, was viewed as expressing God's demand as it manifested itself in the history of the people of Israel.[40]

2. Bultmann is painstakingly careful to avoid being misconstrued as an *antinomian* for whom Christian freedom would be license, or the negation of all demands. The statement "Christ is the end of the law" certainly does not mean that man is released from all demands, but that man has come into a new understanding of the requirement upon him. Paul is far from antinomian in asserting that faith itself is obedience. Bultmann repeatedly quotes Rom. 7:12, that the law is holy, just, and good. *The law intends nothing other than life,* since it points man toward an "ought" instead of allowing him to live under the illusion that he already lives authentically.[41]

Despite their injunctions against legalistic pride, both Jesus and Paul assume the validity of the law; e.g.:

"Think not that I have come to abolish the law and the prophets; I have come not to abolish them but to fulfil them." (Matt. 5:17.)

"You who boast in the law, do you dishonor God by breaking the law?" (Rom. 2:23.)

Jesus' struggle against the law never supposed that the law itself was evil. Rather, he attacked the idea that fulfilling the letter of the law was enough to satisfy the will of God. Jesus preceded Paul in his polemic against a legalistic obedience in which man misuses the law in an attempt to safeguard his own self-righteousness and behind this mask evade the will of God.[42]

3. Here Bultmann's interpretation of Rom., ch. 7, again becomes significant. For the tension that emerges in that chapter between intention and actualization ("for I do not do what I want, but I do the very thing I hate") is an expression of man's fundamental intention to do the good, juxtaposed with the actual bondage of the will which prevents it.[43] *In man's attempt to fulfill the law the dichotomy that emerges between intention and actuality, willing and doing, does not become apparent as such to any standpoint except that of faith.*[44] Bultmann insists that Paul is not, in Rom., ch. 7, autobiographically describing himself, either prior to faith or after faith, but instead is describing the paradox under which the legalist lives, of trespassing the law in his striving to obey it. For in striving for authentic life, the legal man becomes more and more deeply enmeshed in death. In giving up the law, Paul admittedly surrendered that which had been his chief pride and his greatest gain—his fulfillment of the law.[45]

In all this, however, the purpose of the law remains none other than to lead man to authentic life by concretizing the demands of God. The authentic will[46] of man (the "inward man") intends the good, i.e., strives to meet whatever requirements it thinks necessary to achieve authentic life. Paul's assertion that the law is given by God for the sake of transgression must be understood, not from a psychological perspective, but from the perspective of salvation history. The law must enable sin to appear as sin in order that grace can assert its authority.[47]

4. The fundamental self-assertiveness of man appears less in his individual transgressions of the law than in his basic attempt to strive to establish his own righteousness, an effort that roots in his spurious need for recognition and self-glorification. What God requires is that man be ready to live simply by grace alone. Consequently *legalistic man dreads nothing more than God himself*. He dreads the nothing, the *néant*, the supportlessness of God's grace. He dreads the loss of himself, as he understands himself. The natural man thus hates God without knowing it. The real significance of later Jewish legalism for Paul was, in the last analysis, this secret dread of grace, hatred of God, and refusal to live by grace alone.[48]

The insidiousness of the Pharisaic perversion of the law, according to Bultmann, was that it became a means of evading grace. For the devout man who fulfills the law does not need grace. But this is the worst idolatry and false security if the person who strives to fulfill the law simply becomes more deeply implicated in self-righteousness and death.[49]

Paul's specific attack was directed toward striving after righteousness.[50] He did not attack the law in itself, but the perverted self-understanding which was confident that if one obeyed the law, then God could not deny him. Such striving is not limited to Jewish legalism, however, but is the common temptation of all moral men. It is the basic illusion of trying to earn one's own justification, to acquire credit in God's sight. Thus, regardless of whether a man fulfills or transgresses the law, he remains a sinner if his will aims constantly at establishing his own righteousness. Even when he fundamentally intends to do the good, he characteristically wills self-glorification in this intention.[51]

5. The gospel calls men to abandon all self-glorification and to receive the gift of righteousness from God. God's gift alone can establish man's acceptability, since man's striving cannot secure it. This requires radical renunciation, however, of one's desire to gain recognition by one's own adequacy. Such radical renunciation is obedience to the gospel.[52]

That Christ is the end of the law means that he is the end of a life that "lives" by seeking to establish its own righteousness. Christ is the end of that self-understanding which "lives" out of a need for recognition before God, that implies hatred and dread of God's grace. Christ is the end of the law *as* a way of salvation.[53]

The law remains valid insofar as it contains God's demand, but it is disqualified as a means of winning acceptance in God's sight.[54] The relation of the Christian to the law always has a dialectical character: freedom from its demand and yet nonetheless obligation under it. This paradox is formulated in Paul's statement: " 'All things are lawful for me,' but not all things are helpful."[55]

The whole requirement of the law may be summarized as *agapē*. It is in the Christian proclamation, for the first time, that the real intention of the law becomes apparent.

It intends to point us toward our neighbor. Thus from the beginning the true keeping of it would bestow life. The new man is not under the law as a means of salvation, but freely acknowledges himself to be under its fundamental requirement to love the neighbor.[56]

D. RADICAL LOVE AND RADICAL OBEDIENCE

1. In the remaining pages of this exposition we will complete our study of radical obedience by examining the notion "being-for-others" (*Sein-für-den-Anderen*) which Bultmann regards as the presupposition and the consequent of authentic obedience to God. Early in our study we noted that, for Bultmann, *what* the moment demands is in every case *love*.[57] Our present concern is to adumbrate his doctrine of love as a corollary of obedience.

The demand to love is the essential demand of Christian existence. To love means to orient one's whole being purely toward others.[58] Such an orientation is possible only for one who is free from himself, i.e., released from the constant demand to secure his own existence.

Man cannot love, or live purely toward others, unless he understands himself as always already loved in his situation.[59] But his situation is self-assertion. When he is honest with himself he knows that he can have no ultimate confidence in a love that calculates its reward.

Man cannot love until he is already loved by one in whom mistrust is impossible. The only kind of love in which there can be no mistrust is a love that makes itself known as infinitely self-giving. Such is the love of God, according to the Christian proclamation, which is present in every situation in which man is placed.[60]

The only kind of love that could make me truly know that I am loved and thus enabled to love others, says

Bultmann, is one that forgives me in my lovelessness. Such love would have to be the gift of God, since it would be impossible for man as self-assertive sinner to bestow such love. Only an infinite forgiving love could negate one's past and provide estranged man with a real future *for others*.[61]

2. The Christian proclamation declares that such love is always already present in every moment, and that it is made known in the Christ event. It declares that our true existence *with* others is already reestablished juridically and eschatologically in Christ by God's verdict. His love becomes an eschatological event, first as an event concerning Jesus of Nazareth, and then recapitulated in our own history.[62] It is in this way that we love as we have been loved (I John 4:7–11).

Authentic being-for-others is not grounded in man's sheer self-initiated decision to love others, but in response to the infinite forgiving love already shown to him. It is based, not on the optimistic conviction of the goodness of humanity, but on the primordial love of God which is shown in the Christ event.[63]

Such love stands in sharpest contrast to the *superbia* that characterizes the self-understanding of man prior to faith. Bultmann defines sin as the desire of man to be like God (*das Sein-wollen wie Gott*), or the desire to be independent of claims of others.[64] The Christian proclamation meets man in his *superbia* with a word of promise: forgiveness of sin. When men hear and obey this promise, it involves a twofold acknowledgment: a negative acknowledgment that the self does not live to itself but in dependence on God and the neighbor, and a positive acknowledgment that authentic selfhood means *living for the other person*. Thus love completely overturns the

superbia that turns man away from others. Christian faith
has its distinctive character, says Bultmann, in that it
witnesses to an *event* that gives it the *right* to make the
promise of forgiveness to men, the salvation occurrence
in Jesus Christ.[65]

3. The *neighbor* is defined by Bultmann as *"the one who
is always already before me,"* rather than one whom I
first must seek out and find.[66] Christian ethics understands
not that I first go and lay claim on the neighbor, but that
he has already laid claim upon me. It sees the existing
individual as already in a primary I-Thou relation with
the neighbor that cries out for acknowledgment and recognition. The I-Thou relation does not have to be created by
man. On the contrary, man's being is from the outset
being-with-others (*Miteinandersein*).[67]

The question, "Who is my neighbor?" can be raised
only out of a misunderstanding of who the neighbor is,
and more profoundly, a misunderstanding of who oneself
is.[68] For to ask this question is to pretend that the neighbor
is not already before me, and that I could exist without
him. It misunderstands the I-Thou relation as something
that man must first create, rather than acknowledge as
already written into human existence as such.[69]

In the essay *"Das christliche Gebot der Nächstenliebe,"*
Bultmann defines *love* as "that understanding which discloses who my neighbor is, and in doing so discloses what
I ought to do."[70] Love, he says, is an understanding of
myself in an existential covenant with the neighbor in
each situation. Love is not a *general* understanding of my
covenant with man as a whole, but that particular bond
which exists with my fellow human being who encounters
me in the specific situation in which I now exist.[71]

But love can be understood only by loving. We may

characterize it as an activity and attitude directed by an understanding of the self as having its authentic existence *with* others. Although this is love's proper definition, in the last analysis "what love is cannot be understood through the elucidation of the concept of the neighbor, but only through seeing my neighbor as neighbor."[72] We cannot say *what love is.* If a man misunderstands human existence individualistically (as if I could have my being apart from my neighbor), then one cannot by conceptual argumentation make him understand what love is, since love is a way of understanding the relation of I and Thou that is possible only for one who finds himself in this relation.[73] Man is able to understand love only insofar as he knows himself always already to be loved in the situation in which he finds himself, which is precisely what the Christian proclamation is concerned to declare as a reality.

4. Being-for-others is distinguished by Bultmann from the idea of love of humanity-in-general, or the idea of love based on the ultimate dignity of man found in Kant and the Stoics. The basis of this view of love is that there is something intrinsic in man that is worthy of love. The Christian understanding of human existence as existence-with-others is the opposite of this notion that ultimately sees man as individuated. *Being-for-others is not a quality or property that the self possesses and contains within itself, apart from the neighbor.* Rather, it is precisely a way of being with others. Bultmann writes that love is not a *what* (a quality) but a *how* of one's being-with-others.[74]

True love of the neighbor differs from natural impulsive love (*erōs*) in which the self desires an object to enhance itself. True being-for-others requires the total reversal of this erotic direction, since it is based on the false self-understanding that I can enhance myself by exploiting my neighbor.[75] Christian theology knows, however, that if *agapē* requires the reversal of the natural erotic direction of man's inclinations, then it is absurd to believe that other natural men can love me, since they like me are self-assertive. I cannot love others unless I understand myself to be loved, and I cannot reasonably understand myself to be loved by others insofar as I can be sure that the natural *erōs* that I know is present in myself is present in others. Further, I know that my *erōs* is a *selective* love, choosing only those objects to love which will ensure a return.[76] How can I be *for* others, when I know the human situation to be such?

Only that love which is infinitely self-giving and for-giving, which is declared in the gospel, says Bultmann, is able to provide a basis upon which I can be *for* others. In short, I cannot love unless I know myself to be loved, and that I know in the Christ event.[77]

5. The paradoxical dialectic of freedom and obedience is operative in love. For he who is "not under the law himself" chooses herein to become a servant of "those under the law" and "those outside the law."[78] He finds himself called freely to love as he is loved.

The orientation of one's being purely for others is possible only to one who is free from himself. *In being made free from himself, the faithful man is enabled to become free for others.*[79] Love is thus analogous to obedience. Love is an exercise of freedom in which one renounces self-will and becomes obedient to the call of the neighbor. Paul's phrase, "For though I am free from all men, I have made myself a slave to all" expresses this dialectic.[80]

6. Instead of suggesting that the demands of the situation reveal what love is, Bultmann suggests that *love*

reveals what ought to be done in the situation. Bultmann is concerned to answer the question, "What ought I to do?" Formally stated, the answer to this question is always *love*. But if love is wrongly understood as an ideal form of action, as if man's being could be separated from his doing, then love offers no concrete answer.[81]

Bultmann, after the fashion of Kant, does not allow that love can be a material principle (i.e., having content). Rather, he defines love as an understanding of the nature of human existence as *being bound up with others*. It is a practical understanding of the fact that I and my neighbor belong together that discloses the *what* of the action.

Bultmann's understanding of love bears the mark of Kierkegaard's *Works of Love,* just as his view of obedience bears the mark of Kierkegaard's *Fear and Trembling.* Both of these works, interestingly enough, are strongly indebted to Immanuel Kant for their basic perspective on the moral life.[82] Bultmann follows the Kierkegaardian interpretation of the great commandment, "Love thy neighbor as thyself."[83] Kierkegaard suggests that love does not quest for a lovable object, but finds in the object given, lovability. This Kierkegaardian motif is maintained by Bultmann in such statements as, "With a keen and sure eye, love discovers what there is to be done."[84] Kierkegaard's dictum that "an existential system is impossible"[85] is written into Bultmann's ethics in a most thorough manner.

The demand of the moral good is not made evident to me in a system, or an ideal, but confronts me concretely in my meeting with the neighbor. Who is my neighbor? And what must I do for him? This I must perceive for myself at any given time, and it is in love that I am able to do so.[86]

Philosophical ethics should not try materially to answer the question, "What ought I to do?" Bultmann writes, for

only the individual existing in his particular situation can
answer this. The formal answer is love, but the attempt to
answer the question in detail displays a misunderstanding
of human existence, in that it assumes that the ought can
be abstracted out of the particular I-Thou situation of
the moment.[87]

Greek ethics, understanding man after the analogy of
the artist or craftsman, as material or stuff to be formed
in accordance with an ideal condition, regularly makes
this false assumption, Bultmann thinks. Value theory
makes a similar error, in his view, by regarding the
meaning of an action, not in the completed action, but in
what value or good is attained or realized by the action.
It is not what an action *accomplishes* but what it *is* that is
important.

The deeds of the obedient man are not determined by
timeless principles, but man's concrete encounter in time.
Love is not an ethical principle which from time to time
gives definite answers to the question, "What ought I to
do?" On the contrary, it is an eschatological commandment demanding that man should love *whatever* his situation. Both love and obedience demand, not that the self
discover in the moment objects to love, but that the *loving*
self should recognize what the demands of the moment
are.[88]

E. Love and Decision: Gogarten and Heidegger

1. Man's particular being is a possibility of being (*Sein*
is a *Seinkönnen*), which is to say that his being consists
in his choosing of possibilities for himself. It is therefore in
his deciding and acting that man chooses to be who he *is*
and who he becomes. For Bultmann this is another way
of saying that man is a historical, and not merely a natural,
being. *Man's historical existence is characterized by a*

continuing encounter with possibility, in which he may gain or lose himself in the midst of his choosing.[89]

For this view of human existence, Bultmann acknowledges dependence upon two thinkers in particular: Friedrich Gogarten and Martin Heidegger. He weds Gogarten's view of history and Heidegger's view of decision,[90] the union of which may be shown to have considerable influence upon the shape of the ethic of radical obedience.

He is not unaware that Gogarten and Heidegger are quite different at decisive points. The concept of the *neighbor,* e.g., which plays little part in Heidegger's analysis of man, stands for Gogarten as the central factor of the encounter with the Thou which constitutes man's historicity, whereas the concept of *death,* which plays no central role in Gogarten's view of man, stands for Heidegger as precisely that encounter with absolute limitation which constitutes man's historicity (i.e., human existence takes on ultimate decisiveness when confronted by death as the final limiter of life).[91] On the whole, however, Gogarten and Heidegger provide Bultmann's theology with two closely parallel views of human existence.

2. Decision, for Gogarten, is always to be understood in relation to the Thou that confronts one in the neighbor, whereas for Heidegger, decision is essentially a function of selfhood. For Heidegger, admittedly man's concrete situation is always being determined by his having his being *with* other selves (*Miteinandersein*). Likewise for Gogarten, man's decision in relation to the Thou which confronts him is always already simultaneously the laying hold of a possibility of himself.[92] It is in this way that these two interpretations are not precisely the same, but are parallel. These two views are juxtaposed by Bultmann in his doctrines of obedience and love.[93]

What constitutes man's historicity (*Geschichtlichkeit*),

or his existence as a historical being? For Gogarten it is love, and for Heidegger it is decision. Bultmann joins love and decision in his view of radical obedience. By bringing together these two views of historicity, he is able to construct his distinctive ethic which says, "Only where the I in love for the Thou decides is there actual decisiveness."[94] Thus, *man becomes authentically historical in his decision in love and his loving in decision.* To be radically obedient in the moment means to decide for the neighbor, and in doing so, decide for one's authentic self.

3. Such an ethic, however, must go far beyond the purview of formal existential analysis of the ontology of man. The conflation of these two views of historicity thrusts the ethical question into the sphere of the concrete *existenziell* moment in which the neighbor encounters me. As we have said, the realization of genuine decision in love is a possibility offered to man only in the Christian proclamation. Existential analysis can explicate it as a formal possibility, but cannot offer it as a possibility in fact.[95]

One of the most troublesome questions we encountered in understanding radical obedience was "To *whom* or to *what* is one obedient?" Bultmann insists that formal ethical analysis is in principle incapable of specifying the object, or the "whither" (*wozu*) of radical obedience, since the material content of obedience must be left to the moment. Consequently *it is a misinterpretation of the nature of man's historicity (decision and love) to begin one's ethics by looking for the "whither" of obedience.* Obedience is, rather, a way of being (*Seinsweise*) or a "how" of existing which discovers its object only in concrete encounter.[96]

4. The difference that Bultmann recognizes between Heidegger and Gogarten is precisely the gap over which

radical obedience serves as a bridge. According to Heidegger, human existence is finally limited by death (i.e., true decision is only present in encounter with the nothingness of death), whereas according to Gogarten, decision and historicity are limited by the Thou, (i.e., true decision is only present in encounter with the neighbor who is the concrete bearer of God and his demand).[97]

Bultmann juxtaposes these two views by saying that the limitation of death holds true only of that man who does not love his neighbor in radical obedience. It is because we do not see that our neighbor limits us, that death becomes a limitation to us. But for those who know themselves to be loved (which is the central evangelical conviction), it becomes clear that the real limitation of the I is given by the Thou in the concrete meeting with the neighbor, and death thereby has lost its character as a limit.[98] *Death loses its power in the absolute surrender of the self to the demands of the Thou in the meeting with the neighbor,* which, of course, is the definition of radical obedience.

V

CONCLUDING CRITIQUE

THREE CONCERNS occupy our attention in this concluding chapter: (1) focusing the results of our chief
findings in Bultmann, (2) engaging in an internal criticism
of his self-consistency and to a lesser degree an external
criticism of these proposals based on presuppositions different from those held by Bultmann, and (3) inquiring
into the prospects for the future direction of Protestant
ethics. The second of these is our principal concern.

A. REVIEW

1. It is first appropriate that we acknowledge the *difficulty of the task* that Bultmann is trying to accomplish.
His intention has been to propose a radical new approach
for a situational ethic in which the demand of God is
known exclusively in the moment, yet the perception of
the moment is to be determinatively informed by the
Christ event. In his concern not to allow moral knowledge
to be brought to the situation but to emerge only in the
moment, Bultmann has created an anomalous situation
for ethics. For he has virtually been forced to construct
an *ethics against ethics*,[1] i.e., a view of the moral life which
is *against* any view of the moral life that would seek to
systematize the demand of the moment and preimpose
itself upon it.

116

Admittedly, this is a difficult task. But it is all the more difficult when we perceive the larger intention of Bultmann's ethics as the attempt to understand knowledge of God's demand as self-knowledge and authentic self-knowledge as knowledge of God. He would build his ethics on an anthropological axiom which insists that "the question of God and the question of myself are identical."[2] Many problems, such as those of maintaining the transcendence of God and the distinctiveness of the kerygma, spring like the menagerie from Pandora's box from this presupposition.

2. The task would be difficult enough without a crippling restriction that plagues Bultmann's ethics as well as the ethics of a great number of Lutheran and Reformed theologians, viz., *a Kantian pre-understanding of the task of ethics that unconsciously seeks to frame the whole inquiry in the limited language of obedience or obligation.* Bultmann is required by the narrowness of his view of ethics to try to say all that he needs to say about decision, intention, self-knowledge, and freedom in the restricted vocabulary of obedience. It is evident that he gains this limited definition of the moral life primarily from Kant, at least in a much larger measure than from the Biblical witness.

Had Bultmann been able to use a more pluralistic ethical scheme,[3] recognizing various other dimensions of the moral life, such as aspiration and purpose and value, he might have been able to avoid much of his paradoxical, and at times apparently self-contradictory language. Would he need, for example, to speak of man's ontological and ontic situation as a paradox if he interpreted man as a teleological being whose purpose is never factually realized until he knows himself to be loved in his situation? For there is nothing paradoxical in the idea that man has

a purpose that cannot under his present circumstances be
fulfilled, but under other circumstances could.

3. Despite these limitations, however, some rich fruit
has been borne out of this methodology, so before engaging in a critical assessment of these ideas, it would be well
for us to review *the chief findings of our study* in Bultmann and cite his major contributions to contemporary
Protestant ethics.

The findings of this study may be summarized in four
points: (*a*) Bultmann attempts to base an ethics of obedience on a situational understanding of moral knowledge.
(*b*) Insofar as the ontology of man may be existentially
analyzed by an adequate philosophy, it may be seen that
every man knows himself to be under requirement: to *be*
who he *ought* to be, to become an authentic self. To this
extent natural man possesses a certain kind of moral
knowledge in that he knows himself to be under this
requirement. But in his actual estranged situation, he has
always already lost the possibility of becoming who he
ought to be. The actual possibility for authentic life
is given in the address of the Christian proclamation.
(*c*) Radical obedience to God is an actual possibility only
insofar as man knows himself to be always already loved
in his situation with an infinite forgiving love that in effect
bestows upon him a new past and a new future. Such is
the possibility offered once for all in the deed of God in
the Christ event. (*d*) The consequent demand of Christian existence is for radical obedience that hears the
demand of the moment as the demand of God, responding concretely to the neighbor's need as one who has
been loved by God in the Christ event. Man is called in
the moment simply to become who he is as a new creature.
Such a "unity of indicative and imperative" constitutes
the basic principle of ethical interpretation in the New

Testament. These four points constitute the basic themes of the four chapters of our study.

4. Prior to our criticism of these themes, a fitting acknowledgment of some of *Bultmann's major contributions to contemporary Protestant ethics* might include the following points: (*a*) He has provided Christian ethics with a meaningful new perception of the New Testament view of authentic existence. (*b*) He has demonstrated how a *Daseins* ontology can significantly apply to the New Testament understanding of man as a being under requirement. (*c*) He has been an extremely able opponent of legalistic views of obedience without allowing himself to become captive to an antinomian ethic of license. (*d*) He has shown that freedom is a kind of obedience and obedience is a kind of freedom without allowing the two notions to become synonymous. (*e*) He has resolutely tried to pursue his conviction that knowledge of God and self-knowledge are inseparable in an era of theological inquiry in which this assumption has been under vigorous attack. (*f*) His distinction between a formal possibility and a possibility in fact has been highly illuminating in distinguishing philosophical analyses of existence from specifically Christian existence under the Word. (*g*) His clarification of two basic hermeneutical principles, the unity of eschatological and ethical and the unity of indicative and imperative will increasingly be recognized as a significant and enduring contribution to New Testament ethics. And (*h*) his greatest contribution to current Protestant ethics is doubtless his conception of the moment as the bearer of the demand of God.

B. CRITIQUE

Having acknowledged these significant contributions of Bultmann, we have now placed ourselves in a position to bring to bear certain criticisms that have been awaiting expression throughout the preceding pages. As we engage in this critique, we shall limit our comments principally to an internal criticism of the self-consistency of Bultmann's argument, instead of bringing external sources to bear on it. We shall attempt to do little more than try honestly to let Bultmann be a witness against himself insofar as he is inconsistent. Seven points will claim our attention.

1. We have set forth a distinction between Kantian and Biblical patterns of obedience. Since, in the last analysis, the source of the moral demand must be either beyond the self or within the self, these must be understood as mutually exclusive types. The Biblical pattern repudiates the idea that there can be resident moral knowledge within the self, insisting that the demand of God encounters the self from without. The autonomous type rejects the view that the source of the moral demand so transcends the self that it is no longer resident within the rational man. The two types logically exclude each other. They cannot be fused or conflated without logical and semantical difficulties.

Bultmann appears at some points to be maintaining an autonomous ethic, whereas at other points it appears that the moral demand is decisively metonomous (beyond the self). Actually his doctrine of radical obedience is an only partially successful attempt to assert both contradictories. He is dubious of the autonomous alternative because of its temptation to pride and arbitrary self-will and its tendency to subjectify moral knowledge in abstraction from the encounter of the moment. And yet his crucial presupposition that self-knowledge and knowledge of God are inseparable causes him to be uneasy with a thoroughgoing theonomy.

Radical obedience is self-legislative precisely insofar as it demands man's own decision in perceiving the demand of the moment. Bultmann rejects any view of obedience that flees from the responsibility of making this decision, or which would allow some external authority to make man's decision for him. Insofar as such a decision is self-legislated, just to that extent is Bultmann's ethic autonomous.

Radical obedience is not self-legislated, however, but a response to the self-disclosing God insofar as Bultmann says (a) that the demand of the transcendent God is hidden in the demand of the moment (b) that the neighbor encounters the self from without as bearer of this demand; and (c) that the Word of God in the Christ event is not man's natural self-knowledge but God's own self-disclosure.[4]

We have argued that the series of ambiguities and problems in Bultmann's ethical analysis roots back to his key methodological presupposition that authentic self-knowledge is knowledge of God and vice versa. Regrettably, Bultmann has not clarified for his readers either the widespread significance of this presupposition, or the difficulties which proceed from it. The continuing problem in Bultmann's ethics is that *on the one hand he argues that man's knowledge of obligation is self-knowledge and subject to existential analysis; yet on the other hand, he proposes that the unique demand of the present moment constitutes the demand of the transcendent God who is beyond all human grasping, but whose demand is made clear in the event of Christian proclamation and is discernible in the moment.*

The perplexity centers in the fact that at times Bultmann himself bifurcates self-knowledge and knowledge of God, which is the very thing his method protests. Every critique proposed in this section harks back to this methodological inconsistency.

2. The notion that "man knows what is good" is essential to Bultmann's ethic. He goes to great lengths to set forth the idea that God's demand manifests complete discernibility (*Einsichtigkeit*) in the moment. If his argument is found to be vulnerable here, all that follows from it seems vulnerable.

Let us first clarify Bultmann's intention in saying, "Man knows what is good." The parable of the Samaritan is his chief illustration of the idea that all men know what the situation demands when they see the neighbor in need. In asserting that the call of God is unambiguously made known in every moment, Bultmann intends merely to secure a firm foundation for his ethic of obedience, since insofar as a demand is obscure it is in the strict sense unknowable. If the moral requirement is accessible only in the moment, then it must be utterly clear at that nexus if it is to be actualized at all. Thus Bultmann repeatedly argues that since every man knows what it means to love himself, he knows what he ought to do in order to love the neighbor as himself.[5]

Elsewhere in Bultmann's writings, however, he goes into great detail saying exactly the opposite, that the radical fallenness of man prevents authentic moral knowledge and distorts all his good intentions. His superb and sensitive exegesis of Paul's view of bondage to sin and of John's view of the blindness and darkness of the world drives home the point that in man's actual estranged situation he does *not* know what is good, but instead lives constantly out of a false self-understanding.[6] Thus *Bultmann's view of the fallenness of man bears an intolerable witness against much that he has said concerning the discernibility of the demand of God.*

The parable of the good Samaritan is convenient for Bultmann's ethics in this connection, since it speaks of a clear and unambiguous situation of need: an innocent man, beaten and near death beside the road. The parable might be considerably more useful as a central paradigm of man's knowledge of God's demand if it were true that men confront only single unambiguous demands such as this with no conflicts of values. Although admittedly the need of the neighbor confronts us often with greater clarity than we are willing to acknowledge, unfortunately every situation of decision is not as clear-cut and uncluttered as the example of the single needy man beside the road.

Bultmann's ethic envisions no sense of moral ambiguity in the moment of decision. He assumes that the decider may always know precisely what he ought to do in the moment. The obstacle to doing what he ought to do lies exclusively in the will, never in *ignorance* of the good. This seems to be hardly a tenable position, particularly in the light of contemporary political analyses that constantly remind us that our choices are never either good or bad in a wholly unambiguous fashion, but rather always involved in a complex mesh of conflicting values and obligations.[7] In insisting on the clarity of the moral demand, Bultmann is farther removed from the existentialist ethics with which he is often presumed to be associated, and much nearer to a classical Kantian view of clear moral knowledge.

Bultmann's ethic is diluted by the absence of a realistic understanding of the intense and endless *conflicts of values* and interests and obligations that characterize human existence. The Christ event does not transport man out of the realm of such conflicts, but enables him to deal with them in a new way, choosing and negating values in the light of the Word of forgiveness. Bultmann's doctrine of obedience fails to take into account the clash of genuine obligations, the competition of goods-for-me and goods-for-others, the inner struggle of legitimate desires, goals, goods, purposes, loves, strivings, and values that takes place no less in Christian man than in man as such. Bultmann seems only remotely concerned that the special demand of the moment always appears only in competition with other demands. His belief that only one demand confronts man in any given moment cannot be corroborated with our concrete moral experience. Our ready association of our own situation with characters in the contemporary novel or theater who personify man as he is caught in many conflicts of values constitutes a kind of evidence that we know ourselves to be such persons.

Bultmann's crucial assumption of the strict clarity of moral knowledge therefore seems highly dubious, and remains nothing more than an unsupported assertion. It takes little imagination to perceive that the historical rootage of this assumption is the Kantian idea of the a priori moral law in every rational being.

3. A related problem is his assertion that every man knows how to love because he knows how he himself would wish to be loved. Repeatedly his reasoning on the clarity of situational moral knowledge harks back to this assumption that every man is privy to clear knowledge about how he would wish to be affirmed, known, understood, and loved by others. Even the commandment to love others as oneself merely serves the purpose of pointing out to man *that* he ought to love others in the same radical way he already clearly knows how he would happily be loved by them. It does not tell him what to do in order to love, since he already knows that by virtue of

knowing what he would desire others to be and do on his behalf.

However reasonable this sequence of thought may seem, it remains burdened with *a highly questionable premise, viz., that every man knows precisely and clearly how he would wish to be loved by others.* The clinical wisdom of psychotherapy has persuasively called our attention to just how little we know of how to love ourselves properly, and consequently how twisted is our perception of how we would wish to be loved. If we want to be loved possessively, masochistically, dependently, with a love that compensates for our guilts and reassures our anxieties, then how little are we really capable of knowing how we *need* to be loved. How insecure, therefore, is our platform for knowing how to love others!

Karl Menninger's *Man Against Himself*[8] is certainly a horrid enough cacophony of dissonant pathological descriptions to show us the varieties of our ascetic, narcissistic, sadistic, and self-destructive forms of self-relation. It is an equally acceptable axiom for both psychotherapy and theology that man cannot love until he can truly understand himself to be loved. Bultmann affirms this, but does not allow it sufficiently to correct his argument that every man knows how to love others because he knows how he would wish to be loved. Better acquaintance with the psychoanalytic perception of man's inauthenticity would surely have convinced him that man does not enjoy such clear self-knowledge of the kind of love he *needs,* although he may well know what he *desires.*

4. In arguing that the moment contains everything necessary for knowledge of the demand of God, Bultmann defends himself in no way against the charge that the Christian memory brings nothing into the moment.

Yet he repeatedly interprets Christian existence as a mode of action in the moment which is under the determination of the salvation event. *If the Christ event is determinative for Christian existence, then it cannot be maintained that the moment contains everything necessary for knowledge of God's demand,* but rather one must acknowledge a dialogue between the Christian memory on the one hand and the demands of the present moment on the other. Bultmann seems wholly unconcerned with this problem.[9]

Further, Bultmann argues that all standards and norms brought from the past are called into question in the moment. Does he thereby mean that the historical memory of the Christian community and the individual's memory of the salvation occurrence is also called into question? Evidently not, for he acknowledges that it is precisely the Christian proclamation that calls all anthropological standards to question in the moment. But the Christian proclamation is not exclusively an event of the present. It must be brought *to* the present moment from the apostolic and historical Christian witness. Bultmann never introduces his readers to the way in which he conceives of the historical *durability* of the Christian message and self-understanding. Put differently, the problem of *tradition*[10] is neglected in his existentialist eschatology.

It is significant that the meaning he assigns to the Christian proclamation of forgiveness is precisely the annulment of the past! The Christian view of obedience subsumes everything under the category of Now, he suggests. Does he mean by this that there is no historical durability that may be identified from moment to moment and generation to generation, and that man's interest in the past is thereby nullified? Of course not, since much of his labor as a theologian has been devoted to historical (*historisch*) study. In view of this it seems curious, however, that Bultmann would ignore the special problem of historical continuity.

Consequently Bultmann's view of "the moment" is constantly in danger of becoming an abstraction. By abstract, we here mean "to take out of relationality." This is simply to say that a concept of "the moment" that is separated from its historical relatedness, its contextual eventfulness, its place in relation to the past and future, no longer displays the concreteness that is sometimes claimed for it, but rather becomes abstract. The whole range of moral action, obligation, purposing, loving, striving, and evaluating cannot be squeezed into the narrow confines of the category "Now," but requires a more inclusive view of time.

Bultmann distinguishes Christian obedience from all *Weltanschauungen*, suggesting that the former is open to every unique moment, whereas the latter seeks refuge and security from decision in generalization, or by making the instant a case of the general. One can hardly escape a world view, however, in the sense in which Bultmann defines the term, since in order to reflect, one must stand back from the immediacy of the moment and engage in generalization. Bultmann himself seems to propose an alternative world view, according to his own definition, in his understanding of the Christian proclamation, inasmuch as he insists that authentic obedience to God requires that man "stand under the determination of the Christ event."

5. Bultmann has taken the position that when natural man in his fallenness speaks of the knowledge of God's demands, what he really *knows* is himself. He possesses self-knowledge of his own human situation of limitation

and finitude, and knowledge that he is not what he ought to be; but such knowledge is not, properly speaking, knowledge of God.

On the other hand, however, he has declared with equal emphasis that self-knowledge and knowledge of God are inseparable. In his exegesis of Paul's view of conscience, he declares that "the demand which conscience apprehends is grounded in a transcendent sphere over against man," and that it constitutes an "objective witness" within the ontology of man to the demand of God. This is genuinely ambiguous, and no matter how closely inspected, it does not resolve itself.

Again, he holds that an existential knowledge of God is present in man's search for happiness and meaning, but on the other hand holds that such knowledge is merely a sort of anticipative knowledge, and nothing more, in the last analysis, than self-knowledge, and not to be confused with God's revelation, which is everywhere hidden, but made known in Jesus Christ.

Or again, to state the ambiguity sharply, *man as such has knowledge of God, whether consciously or unconsciously, in his knowledge of himself as a being under limitation and requirement but the object of his knowledge is not God but himself.* As we have suggested earlier, Bultmann seems determined to trap himself in the simplest logical self-contradiction by saying that the object of self-knowledge is God, and yet is not God.

Is Gerhardt Kuhlmann's charge a proper one, that Bultmann's use of Heidegger amounts to a profanization of revelation? Or on the other hand, is the case exactly the reverse, that Bultmann's interest is so overwhelmingly theological, and concerned with an intelligible interpretation of revelation, that he seizes Heidegger's language and anthropological analysis and uses it as a mere tool for the service of Christian theologizing? As we have previously suggested, Bultmann's interests run in two directions which stand in constant tension: existential analysis of the ontology of man, and the clarification of the kerygma as God's address to existing man. Against either the interpretation that Bultmann's determinative concern is existentialist philosophy,[11] or the opposite view that his overriding theological interests cancel out possible dialogue with the philosophical community,[12] it seems evident that these are parallel interests which cannot be separated or superordinated and subordinated. And as has been suggested, this methodological doubleness rests upon the crucial presupposition that self-knowledge and knowledge of God cannot be bifurcated.

6. Bultmann's man of obedience, much like Kant's (and yet so different with respect to the nature of the imperative), does not exist self-consciously in a durable history, with a temporal series of moments in a continuous procession. Kantian obedience is thoroughly nonhistorical. Bultmann's radical obedience is historical only with respect to the present, but nonhistorical with respect to duration. For Bultmann, history is circumscribed by the now-moment. Only one moment is truly "historical" and that is "Now." Thus, in a certain sense, Bultmann *dehistoricizes man.*

It is in this respect that the Biblical view of obedience differs so radically from Bultmann's view. In the Bible, man's response to God exists only in the context of a *durable* history, i.e., a history that displays genuine continuity with the past, and that lives out of the past (as the people of Israel lived out of the exodus history) and toward the future (as Israel lived toward the Day of the

Lord). This is to be distinguished from that view which
circumscribes history within the "Now."

Without this covenantal history, Biblical obedience
would be hopelessly abstract. The remembered historical
and existential realities of deliverance and covenant form
the basis for the gratitude out of which Israel lived and
understood obedience. In the Biblical view of obedience,
the past remains real and is not annihilated or overcome.
Past, present, and future have a realism of their own. Old
and New Testament writers respect this realism. As a
matter of fact, in the Bible the demands of the moment
are interpretable only in the light of the remembered
historical and existential realities of deliverance and covenant. Israel regarded these events as truly *past*, and yet
truly impinging on the present and the future.

One might state the distinction quite simply in this
way: in the Bible the demand does not have to be given
anew in each particular situation. It was assumed that
God's demand possessed continuity and historical durability. For Bultmann, on the other hand, it is assumed that
the demand of God is uniquely given anew in each moment. The significance of the law for the covenant community of Israel was that the requirement of God had the
character of historical durability and continuity from
moment to moment. But this is precisely the distinctive
aspect of Bultmann's ethics: he rejects any notion of obedience that does not attend exclusively to the unique
demand of the present moment.

7. Our principal critique of Bultmann's doctrine of obedience, however, is yet to be made explicit. It is our objec-
tion to what we will call his basic tendency to "anthropologize" the relation between God and man. In another
context we might speak of Barth's opposite tendency to

"Christologize" the relation between God and man.[13] In both cases the idea of obedience to God is impoverished by the loss of one or the other of the two personal subjects in live dialogical encounter which we find in the Biblical witness.

Bultmann's doctrine of radical obedience so turns our attention to the self in the moment that the Lord of the self and the moment becomes merely a predicate of the self in the moment. This is what is meant by Bultmann's tendency to anthropologize the relation between God and man. *Just as God became the mere "Whence" of Schleiermacher's feeling of absolute dependence,*[14] *the divine Subject becomes the mere "Whence"* (Woher) *of Bultmann's understanding of the demand of the moment.* The divine Subject is relegated to the status of a predicate of the demand encountered by the self in the moment. The free sovereign Lord is depersonalized by the identification of his will with the demand of the moment. For it is only by some stretch of the imagination that we can regard the moment as a free personal agent.

In his concern to avoid mythological language in speaking of the demand of God, Bultmann has had to take a position that secularizes the demand and depersonalizes the One who makes the demand. In this respect his understanding of obedience falls short of the dialogical relationship so evident in the Biblical witness, and which might properly be viewed as the basic framework of an integral Protesant understanding of obedience to God.

C. WHITHER PROTESTANT ETHICS?

Having set forth and critically analyzed the basic features of an existential-eschatological ethic, we now might properly ask about possible directions which we

might hope or expect that subsequent Protestant ethics
might take in the future. How can the achievements of
Bultmann's ethic be elaborated, corrected, and tran-
scended without either reduplicating his efforts or becoming further enmeshed in some of his inadequacies?
Although we would presume to do no more than make a
few possible suggestions, realizing that more could be
significantly added, several possible alternatives seem to
represent special need or promise.

1. A needed elaboration of radical obedience is some
firm reaffirmation of the relevance of the law amid the
life of Christian freedom, perhaps giving fresh attention
to the traditional Protestant concept of the three uses of
the law,[15] especially its third use, in order to avoid the
antinomian temptations in contextual ethics (which Bultmann himself clearly tries to avoid)[16] and to give more
concrete guidance for perception of the demand of God
in the moment. Reinhold Niebuhr's critique of Barth's
ethics[17] holds equally true for Bultmann, that its situational character suffers from a lack of principle which in-
creases the temptation toward capricious moral judgments. If every event must be judged afresh and without
any principle or durable mode of perception of moral
judgments, then everything rests upon the capacity of sinful self-assertive man to perceive God's clear demand in
the moment, admittedly a very insecure base.

Consequently something further needs to be said about
the importance of the law as a guide to the Christian life
without fundamentally denying either the contextual character of moral judgments or the freedom for which Christ
has set us free. Although perhaps the contributions of
John Bennett and Alfred de Quervain[18] have been more
valuable than any other in the search for median princi-

ples, we cannot wish to see Protestant ethics revert either to a casuistry[19] or an ambiguous theory of natural law.[20] The proper *modus vivendi* between situational ethics and legal principle has not been achieved in our time.

The persistent antinomian inclinations of current Protestantism toward an ethic of self-affirmation without self-denial, gospel without law, freedom without obedience, and grace without obligation constitutes perhaps the most urgent problem of Protestant ethics, which, if we fail to clarify in the next decades, may make it necessary for us to unlearn much that we have learned about "Christian liberty." Perhaps the emerging conversation with Roman Catholicism, long steeped in an ethic of law and virtue, will provide some clues for the overcoming of these antinomian temptations without debilitating the accomplishments achieved in the last two generations in freeing us from a legalistic perception of the demand of God.

2. One area of current Protestant ethics that requires and deserves more refinement and elaboration is the enterprise of a *theology of culture*, already well-initiated by Tillich, i.e., the process of analyzing cultural expressions such as art, music, literature, architecture, philosophy, psychotherapy, etc., with respect to the ultimate concerns and centers of value which are there being expressed. That Bultmann's existential analysis, hermeneutics, and demythologizing have considerable relevance for a theology of culture has largely gone unnoticed, perhaps because Bultmann has not seemed to notice it himself.

The chief inadequacy of Tillich's work thus far has been his limited preoccupation with estrangement and the old man. Bultmann has achieved a sharper clarification of the character of authentic human existence. The concepts of essence and new being, so ambiguous in Tillich, could be

demythologized and better clarified by Bultmann's description of authenticity. Tillich and Bultmann share a
profound concern to discover and forge a language that
will speak meaningfully to the contemporary mind, but
Bultmann offers a more viable perception of everyman's
fundamental intention (however perverted) for authentic
existence which could be most useful in further explicat-
ing the forms of cultural self-expression that Tillich is so
concerned to understand theologically. Tillich can see in
Picasso's *Guernica,* for example, only "the human predicament in our period, . . . a world of guilt, anxiety, and
despair,"[21] whereas with the *Daseins* analytic that Bultmann provides we can also see in *Guernica* the striving
of man for authenticity amid the utter collapse of all
normal reliances.

Furthermore, Tillich's interest in a theology of culture
has tended to neglect "popular culture," folk music, the
cinema, choreography, cartoon satire, jazz, etc., limiting
his analysis to the great tradition and the growing edge of
artists and cultural expressions. Perhaps the new ground
that is yet to be cultivated is a far more serious analysis
of the ultimate concerns being expressed mythologically
in mass media and folk culture, which may tell us as much
about ourselves as does the growing edge.

3. Another promising direction of further elaboration is
a new look at *value theory* from the vantage point of
existential analysis and *Daseins* ontology. Value analysis
as a distinctive method and language for dealing with
man's moral existence constitutes a neglected and needed
addendum to existentialist ethics. The rich tradition of
value theorists identified with the names of Ralph Barton
Perry, John Dewey, and Nicolai Hartmann in this century, and in an earlier period with Scheler, Ritschl, Lotze,

and many of the Hegelians has been disastrously neglected by contemporary ethicists. A new attempt at a phenomenology of values following along the lines of Nicolai Hartmann,[22] but with some of the correctives that have already been suggested by H. Richard Niebuhr, could be a most significant and promising extension of the eschatological-existential-kerygmatic base that Bultmann has laid for Protestant ethics.

To Charles Hartshorne's social theory of value[23] and Richard Niebuhr's relational theory of value[24] needs to be added a broader new study of the range and variety of competing values, and their relation to the problem of guilt and forgiveness. Some sharpened clarification of the nature of conflicts of values is also needed in the light of the alleged clarity of the Word of God in the moment. The distinction between God, the gods, and values, somewhat unclear in the work of Richard Niebuhr, needs further refinement and development, as well as the relation of Christian faith of value judgments, never adequately set forth by the Ritschlians.

4. A related possible direction for subsequent Protestant thought is toward a new form of *rapprochement* between *psychotherapeutic and ethical insight*. More specifically, value-theology and valuational ethics have never really had their conversation with psychotherapeutic counseling. It is unfortunate that Bultmann's ethic has been influenced by Heidegger without also being shaped by Binswanger,[25] Sullivan,[26] and Rogers.[27] Regrettably he has limited his anthropological analysis to a *Daseins* ontology without awareness of the impressive potentialities of existential psychoanalysis and American client-centered therapy.

How might we expect the conversation between counseling and ethics fruitfully to emerge in the light of the

Bultmannian contribution? The clinical perception of neurosis is as significant an alternative for understanding anxiety and guilt (which Bultmann can only grapple with in Heideggerian categories) as the therapeutic process is for nurturing sick men toward actualizing in some measure authentic existence (a task, which, according to Bultmann, philosophy is ill-advised to attempt). The ontic limitations involved in actualizing authentic historicity may be thoroughly demonstrated in the process of neurotic self-idealization. Karen Horney's description of the compulsive character of the idealized self-image[28] constitutes an amazing parallel and elaboration of Bultmann's description of *Eigenmächtigkeit*. And if psychotherapy can refine much that Bultmann has said about inauthenticity, much more can it also assist in setting forth the ontological and ontic possibilities of authentic human existence that are only partially clarified by Bultmann in complex Heideggerian language. Carl Rogers' description of "the fully functioning person" is a particularly significant contribution in this connection.[29]

5. The rapidly emerging ecumenical dialogue, particularly the potentially volatile conversation between *Roman Catholics and Protestants*, may hold special significance for post-Bultmannian ethics. Undoubtedly Protestants are just as inadequately prepared for this as post Vatican II Romans. Since Roman Catholic moral theory from Saint Thomas on has cultivated a special language and way of framing questions, Protestants must increasingly become familiar with that language if genuine dialogue is to emerge.

What is the feasibility of meaningful *Auseinandersetzung* between the existentialist-eschatological-Lutheran tradition and the substantialist-rationalist-Catholic tradition in ethics? It first needs to be pointed out that already significant dialogue exists between the avante-garde Roman Catholic theologians and the post-Bultmannian scholars scattered across Europe, to which the work of Heinrich Schlier,[30] Hans Küng,[31] and Karl Rahner[32] bears impressive witness. Although most of the traditional Thomist categories in law and ethics as well as metaphysics and epistemology have been rejected by existential theology, Thomism is unquestionably undergoing very rapid transformation and we shall even venture to say "demythologization." Furthermore a vigorous new Augustinianism is appearing in Roman Catholic theology, making Thomism hardly an exclusive voice, if it ever was. It is primarily with this Augustinian tradition that the conversation has emerged and will be nurtured. Although it would be more than foolhardy to venture to predict what might be ahead in this dialogue, at least it must be cited as an immensely promising one for Protestant ethics.

6. Post form-critical Biblical studies are due for a fresh encounter with the perennial questions of *Biblical ethics,* a subject which, in the last thirty years since the demise of liberal treatments of the ethics of the prophets and Jesus, has been virtually ignored with few exceptions. Perhaps the ethics of Jesus will again be the touch point for such a development, although it seems impossible that such a discussion could ground itself in a pre form-critical confidence in the picture of the historical Jesus or any other Jesus than he who was remembered by the proclaiming church as Savior and Lord. Both the principles of the interrelation of the eschatological and ethical and the unity of the indicative and imperative need to be put to work in actual exegetical studies. They are sharp tools and need further application.

7. Although it is generally admitted that a more genuine dialogue is needed between *Anglo-American and Continental* ethical traditions than has yet been achieved, the form and content of that conversation is yet to be chosen. The characteristic Anglo-Saxon approach to ethical issues has been inductive, moving as does English law from particular cases to broader principles, whereas the characteristic Continental approach has been deductive, like Roman and Teutonic legal traditions, moving from first principles of law to particular cases. This contrast is rooted deeply in the respective differences between the two cultural histories. As the empiricists from Hume to the logical analysts have been the chief shaping figures of modern British ethics, so the systematic moral philosophers from Kant to Heidegger have been the determinative voices in modern Continental ethics.

Each with a distinctive ethos, these cultural histories need patiently and clearly to speak to and listen to one another. Admittedly they have always been in some sort of conversation, but they have never really listened as empathetically as they might. We cannot agree either with those who assert that American theology is fully prepared to fly with its own wings and cut its roots loose from European dependencies, or with those who wish this conversation to be a mere monologue with our echoing and shadowing the German academic tradition. Doubtless the vitality and depth of the German academic tradition has proved sufficiently rich that German scholars have neglected important contributions and developments from our side, not the least of which has been the work of H. Richard Niebuhr, whose contributions are rarely quoted in German sources. Admittedly American monolingual limitations have made it difficult for us to engage in genuine dialogue with those who most need us and whom we most need. Nowhere is this drought more evident than in the area of Christian social ethics where American thought still seems to be experiencing a disruptive lack of clear self-identity and hunger for new rootage, and yet either we cannot or do not read the exciting new developments on the Continent largely represented by the contributors to *Foi et Vie, Die Mitarbeit,* and *Zeitschrift für Evangelische Ethik.* American ethical thought has too long been in a now rebellious, now dependent relation vis-à-vis the Continent, and needs increasingly to speak out of its own matured experience, hopefully without the loss of genuine communication with our companions abroad. Just as a new word needs to be spoken in Anglo-American ethics about the clarity of the Word of God, so a corrective Anglo-American word needs to be spoken to Continental deontological exclusivism. Among American ethicists only Richard Niebuhr has led the way in this, as in so many other respects, and it deserves notice that most of the possible directions we might now propose for a post-Bultmannian development in Protestant ethics have already been begun by him.

8. Finally we cannot fail to mention that Bultmann's view of radical obedience has astonishing relevance for the doctrine of *vocation,* which so urgently needs to be clarified in contemporary Christian social ethics. Doubtless the growing edge of the church's life today, alongside ecumenical developments, is the experimental approach to Christian *koinōnia, diakonia,* and dialogue in lay communities in which a new perception of Christian vocation is being achieved. The most exciting dimension of the current work of the World Council of Churches is the Department on the Laity.[33] The recovery of the ministry

of the laity has promise of reshaping the church.

Yet it is sad but necessary to say that despite the renewal of the laity, one of the most neglected issues of Protestant ethics is vocation. What definitive constructive treatment of vocation may be cited in English in the last twenty-five years, since Robert Calhoun's *God and the Common Life?*[34] Although the problem of vocation remains the most vacuous arena of current Protestant ethics, none can deny that its clarification is required with accelerating urgency in a rapidly technologizing society.

Radical obedience as a situational perception of the calling of God in the moment is unavoidably related to the basic issues of vocational self-understanding and self-fulfillment. One direction in which current Protestant ethics urgently needs to move in response to Bultmann's achievement is toward a new discussion of vocation rooted in an eschatological perception of history, taking into consideration the striking new developments in the experimental lay communities of prayer, study, and service.

RESPONSE

By Rudolf Bultmann

I HAVE READ with great interest your study of the idea of obedience in contemporary Protestant ethics. You have quite clearly articulated the problem of the correct understanding of ethical obedience. The carefulness and objectivity of your discussion is commendable, as well as the fact that your presentation is interwoven with critical judgments. I now have some critical thoughts of my own to set against your conclusions.

Your analysis of the Biblical and Kantian patterns of obedience is a good introduction to the framing of the problem. But since in your whole presentation the question of the source of authority that calls man to obedience is decisive—especially whether there is a transcendent authority to which man owes obedience—I would wish that you would also ask of the Greeks, and especially of Plato, How does Plato understand the relation of man to a transcendent power? Especially, in what sense does Plato know of a transcendent sphere?

I have some thoughts in opposition to your characterization of Biblical ethics. You correctly distinguish the formal ethic of legalism. But is the distinction between "metonomous" and "autonomous" correct? Can there be a third category outside of heteronomy and autonomy? You wish to distinguish the ethic of the metonomous from autonomy in such a way that the metonomous ethic depends upon the recognition of a transcendent authority that stands beyond man. But must not also Kant's ethic be denoted as metonomous in this sense? For even it hinges on the recognition of an authority that transcends the empirical man. According to Kant, the ethical demand speaks to the empirical man: "Thou shalt!" Whether the speaking authority is regarded as a person (as in the Bible) or as an impersonal law (as in Kant) is rather a matter of indifference as concerns the definition of obedience. A "dialogue" can be spoken of only in an artificial sense in the Bible as well as Kant. The "answer" to the command is in both cases the obedient act of man.

Since according to Kant the empirical man is at the same time a rational being, and since the ethical command is a command of reason, then one can call his ethic autonomous, insofar as man can understand the command as given by himself. The authority that he as empirical man must obey is not thereby repudiated.

Furthermore, since man realizes his freedom in obedience and thereby wins his authenticity, one can say of the Kantian ethic precisely what you say of the Biblical ethic, that deontology lives out of soteriological self-understanding, since this does not need to be in opposition to "rational self-understanding."

Now you suggest that this is precisely the essential distinction between the Kantian ethic and the Bible, that the Bible knows nothing of an empirical man and a rational man, but that the Bible knows only the *whole* man who stands under the authority of God. I cannot agree with this. The Bible has *only* the empirical man in view and knows nothing of the rational man at all. The Bible ignores the rational and therefore is unable to know anything of the concept of autonomy in Kant's sense. But this concept does not necessarily stand in contradiction to the Bible.

If there cannot be a third position apart from autonomy and heteronomy, there remain three possibilities: (1) the ethic of the Bible is heteronomous, or (2) it must be implicitly autonomous, or (3) it is part heteronomous, part autonomous.

The third seems to me to be the case. The Biblical ethic is heteronomous insofar as it consists of cultic and ritual writings that can actually only be fulfilled "legalistically" and thus "heteronomously." But that the Biblical ethic is also implicitly autonomous (in a hidden way) is shown in the fact that alongside the legalistic demands and in opposition to them stand genuine ethical demands like the demand of the prophets for law and justice (cf., e.g., Micah 5:6–8) and Jesus' struggle against the legalism of the scribes. But it further shows itself to be autonomous in connection with the motivation of the demand by reference to history, wherein you (correctly) perceive a distinction between Biblical and Kantian ethics. For, according to the Old Testament understanding, history itself reveals God's law and justice, and insofar as he understands history and himself in history, man must take upon himself the demand of law and justice, and in this sense he is autonomous. Whereas according to Kant, man is autonomous thanks to his reason; according to the Bible, man is such thanks to his understanding of history.

The genuine difference between Kant and the Bible is therefore not the distinction between "metonomy" and autonomy, but that for Kant the authentic nature of man is rational, whereas for the Bible it is historical.

The other distinctions you enumerate are either not entirely true distinctions, since they in my opinion are based partly upon a misconception of autonomy, or they hark back to the aforementioned distinction.

Your presentation of my view of obedience is carefully done and essentially right (note especially the sections on "being and doing," "deed and work," "what the moment demands," and "formal possibility and possibility in fact"). However, I cannot concede that I "anthropologize" the relation between God and man if I say that the moment (the Now) receives the demand of God. The moment is not at all the product of human subjectivity, but an occurrence demanding decision. In the moment one meets the *transcendent* divine demand in the attire of *concrete* obligation. Nor can I concede that the "anthropological analysis of the process of the recipiency of the Word in the situation of concrete encounter in the moment" impairs the thought of obedience, since my "anthropology" is not that of Feuerbach, which recognizes nothing over against man.

You find in my thinking a contradiction that says on the one hand that man knows what the good is, but on the other hand says that the sin of man prevents his perception of the good and perverts his "good intentions." In this connection, you bring to my attention a paradox that I might well have pointed out more explicitly.

If sin is not a natural quality of man, but an offense for which man is responsible, then the precondition of sin is that man knows the good—perhaps I should say, man *may* know the good. For to know the good is a possibility that essentially belongs to human existence; but also to such existence belongs the possibility of repressing this perception of the good or of bringing it only relatively into awareness. The (possible) knowledge of requirement must realize itself in the (factual) acknowledgment of the concrete act. Until it is brought into full awareness, the paradox holds true: that man has the knowledge of the good, and yet he does not have it.

If there is "moral ambiguity in the moment of decision," then such is the result of not having realized the possibility of knowing the good. The "conflicts of values and interests and obligations" (p. 123) characterize human existence as sinful. Therefore, obedience will always take place as *decision* between concrete possibilities. However, decision means the choice to hear *one* command as the divine requirement out of the multitude of voices of concrete commands. These are *as such* never divine demands, and man can never be *certain* whether he has heard rightly. Thus Luther's *pecca fortiter, sed crede fortius* holds true.

You discovered one of my unsolved problems (p. 125): on the one hand I say that "the Christian memory brings nothing into the moment," but on the other hand I speak of Christian existence as "a mode of action in the moment that is under the determination of the Christ event." Such a contradiction may be easy to resolve. To be sure, "the Christian memory" brings nothing into the moment insofar as it is the moment of a *requirement,* i.e., the Christian faith does not constitute the demand as the demand of the moment. But the Christian faith sees every moment in the light of the "Christ event," in the sense that the Christ event teaches man to *know himself* and above all to know himself as one loved by God, so that henceforth he is able as one who is loved to perceive the unambiguous meaning of the demand of God in the concrete situation. To be sure, this knowledge is never secure in itself. But the believer can act, even if his action is a *peccare* as long as he fulfills the *crede fortius.*

You suggest that I ignore historical continuity and reduce the moment to an abstraction (p. 127). But have I not often said that the moment has its significance only in relation with the past and the future? Only in this sense can the Now confront us with the question of decision, since man is in each case now responsible for the past as for the future. The decision as such is always for or against concrete possibilities emerging out of history. It is necessary to question critically the inheritance of the past as to whether and how far the inheritance of the past is a blessing or a curse. And the future stands before decision as the realm of possibilities for responsible action.

With such decision man himself is at the same time deciding for or against himself as he comes out of his past. And insofar as he is thus deciding, he suspends his past in order to appropriate himself anew.

This holds true fundamentally for all men. But the believer knows that human freedom is only something relative, since man himself cannot really make himself free from himself as he emerges out of his past, but he only first becomes genuinely free through the Word of God's forgiveness.

The believer certainly possesses a "memory of the Christ event," but this has no continuity in the *particular* sense that the freedom given him through the Christ event might become a secured possession or a quality of the believer. Faith must be grasped ever anew in ever new hearing of the Word of forgiveness. Must not the prayer of forgiveness be spoken every day? The continuity of world history is something other than the continuity of the Word of God upon which the sinner can rely.

I will not go into further detail in your whole explication, but will mention only a few further points.

Your presentation of Barth's "Christological obedience"[1]

seems to me to be quite good. I would object, however, to Barth's tendency to confuse obedience to the ethical command with the obedience of faith (*hupakoē pisteōs*, according to Paul). As concerns obedience to the ethical command, it is impossible to say "that God has taken responsibility for man."[2] But the faithful man believes that God has freed him in *this* sense from "responsibility," that he is forgiven of his sin and that he thus as sinner is declared righteous. This demand of faith (which is at the same time a gift) does not spring out of the ethical situation and should not be confused with obedience to the ethical demand. It is much more the faith in the Word of forgiveness proclaimed to man and in this sense, it is Christologically grounded. In *this special* sense, it is correct to say: "The imperative that man addresses to himself cannot amount to the command of God."[3]

Such faith is, of course, not a limitation of human freedom, but presupposes its possibility and realization. In *this* sense, freedom for God and obedience to God are the same. And in *this* sense, self-knowledge and knowledge of God are inseparable, since man first knows himself truly in faith. Since Barth confuses ethical obedience and the obedience of faith, he also confuses the freedom of decision that presupposes the ethical command and freedom of God.

It would lead too far if I would wish now to enter into a critique of Barth's concept of *being* and discuss the relation of being and doing. I must content myself with having made these few remarks and will close with my grateful acknowledgment that you have dealt with the problem of Christian obedience so instructively.

RUDOLF BULTMANN

NOTES

ABBREVIATIONS

E & F	*Existence and Faith*	*KD*	*Kirchliche Dogmatik*
Essays	*Essays Philosophical*	*KM*	*Kerygma und Mythos*
	and Theological	*TNT*	*Theologie des Neuen*
G.u.V.	*Glauben und Verstehen*		*Testaments*
		Urchr.	*Das Urchristentum*

PREFACE

1. Gerhardt Kittel, *Theologisches Wörterbuch zum NT* (Stuttgart: Verlag von W. Kohlhammer, 1949), Erster Band, article on *akoē*, pp. 215 ff.

2. As the Greek *akouō* (to hear) and *hupakouō* (to obey) illustrate the close relationship between hearing and obeying, and as the Latin *oboedire* may be translated either to listen or to perform the bidding of another, likewise the German verb *hören* (to hear) is the root word for *Gehorsam* (obedience). Originally the English word "obedience" was, significantly enough, the present participle (*oboediens*) of an ancient French Latin conflation of *ob* (on account of) and *audire* (to hear).

INTRODUCTION

1. It seems ironic that the very moral paralysis from which Reinhold Niebuhr sought to deliver us has been unconsciously compounded by his overriding concern for discriminating moral judgments.

2. Reinhold Niebuhr, *Moral Man and Immoral Society* (Charles Scribner's Sons, 1932).

3. Thomas C. Oden, "Is the Demand of God Ambiguous? An American-European Dialogue," *The Ecumenical Review*, XIII, No. 2 (Jan., 1961), p. 153.

4. *Ibid.*, p. 153.

5. Reinhold Niebuhr is perhaps the preeminent American example of the dualism that Bonhoeffer rejects as "thinking in terms of two spheres." For shot through Niebuhr's entire endeavor is radical duality between God and man, absolute love and proximate justice, moral man and immoral society, etc. Bonhoeffer's critique of such thinking is urgently needed among moralists who are tempted to talk as if man and the world could be understood in an autonomous sense apart from the self-disclosing God. For Bonhoeffer we must never talk about God as if he were out on the edge of human existence, but in terms of his reality at the center of human existence, a theme that F. D. Maurice set forth with great vitality in the mid-nineteenth century. Whenever we think in terms of two spheres of God *and* the world, we fail to understand the God who engages himself in a concrete relation to the world and the world that cannot avoid a concrete relation with God. That God has chosen to be present amid the world is the meaning of the incarnation.

6. Reinhold Niebuhr speaks of the command of love as "an impossible ethical ideal" as if to exclude the possibility of clear here and now response to the claim of God, which is the very center of Bultmann's understanding of radical obedience to God. Niebuhr's thoroughgoing emphasis on the ambiguity of God's requirement tends to undercut the kind of moral certainty that is necessary for decisive moral action. It tends to discourage, debilitate, and unnerve deliberate moral resolution. His emphasis on expertise in moral judgments, which inevitably demands special knowledge of the multiplicity of fact and the need for being in a special nexus for knowing and balancing all the competing interests before one is prepared to make highly discriminating moral decisions, tends to ignore the viability of an ethic of simple wisdom that listens for the Word of God calling in the now, a view that long before Bonhoeffer's call for "simple obedience" was the crux of Bultmann's ethics.

7. Perhaps the deepest problem of contemporary Christian ethics is to discover again the interrelationship between law and gospel. Much Protestant ethical thought tends to fall either into an antinomian ethic of license in which grace is mistaken

for irresponsibility, or toward a moralism that never really takes seriously the freedom for which Christ has set us free. Bultmann has presented us with a very forthright defense against antinomianism, and yet with the most radical conception of freedom under grace, Bultmann's formulation of the interrelation of indicative and imperative and the internal unity of eschatological and ethical has promise of becoming an enduring contribution to Christian moral reflection.

8. See *The Ecumenical Review*, XIII, No. 2 (Jan., 1961), pp. 153 ff., for explication of an argument that attempts to show that the demand of God is clear, however ambiguous the moral decisions of estranged men may seem.

9. A corollary problem in contemporary Protestant ethics is the lack of a definitive formulation of the appropriate relationship between philosophy and theology. Modern Protestant ethics has tended either to reject philosophy altogether or to become diluted in a philosophizing-psychologizing-sociologizing direction. Theological ethics has proved either all too ready or not ready enough to listen to man's own wisdom about himself apart from the Biblical witness. Bultmann's achievement of a new formulation of the relation between philosophy and theology may become a most useful guideline in ethical analysis for establishing both boundaries and dialogue. It is precisely Bultmann's achievement that, despite a multitude of critics of the right, he has made excellent use of existential analysis in understanding man as a moral being under requirement without identifying such analysis with the Christian proclamation, and despite critics of the left, has reasserted the significance of the kerygma without allowing it to become absorbed in modernity. Later we will see how Bultmann's crucial distinction between the ontological and the ontic possibilities of man enables him to effect a new *rapprochement* between theological and philosophical thought, without allowing either one to be absorbed by the other.

10. Ernst Käsemann, "Probleme der Neutestamentlichen Arbeit in Deutschland," *Die Freiheit des Evangeliums und die Ordnung der Gesellschaft*, Beiträge zur Evangelische Theologie, XV (1952), pp. 138 ff.; Hermann Diem, *Dogmatics* (The Westminster Press, 1959), pp. 1–81, 240 ff.

11. Even the ultraconservative schools of American fundamentalism hardly constitute an exception. For even here where one would expect an ethic delimited by exegesis, there has been a "head in the sands" attitude toward the growing edge of exegesis. The eschatology of Albert Schweitzer is still looked upon with paranoic suspiciousness, and there has been little advance beyond a defensive stance toward the achievements of liberal historical criticism.

12. Martin Luther, "The Freedom of a Christian" (1520), *Martin Luther, Selections*, ed. by John Dillenberger (Doubleday & Company, Inc., 1961). John Calvin, *Institutes of the Christian Religion* (London: James Clarke & Company, Ltd., 1953), especially Books II and IV.

13. Schleiermacher's principal ethical works include *Monologe* (1800), *Grundlinien einer Kritik der bisherigen Sittenlehre* (1803), *Entwurf eines Systems der Sittenlehre* (1835), and *Die christliche Sitte nach den Grundsätzen der evangelischen Kirche* (1843).

14. It is perhaps due to his apologetic beginning point that Tillich has become so preoccupied with the old man, human estrangement, the brokenness, *hubris*, and alienation of man. Although this has been his greatest contribution, Bonhoeffer's critique of such thinking seems relevant, that it is not in the boundary situation or in some special *kairos* that the world encounters God, but at the very center of human existence and saturated throughout the whole process of history.

15. Hardly has his philosophical language and method remained simply functional, e.g., with respect to his concept of essence, but instead it has become determinative for *what* he says about man, not merely how he says it.

16. Paul Tillich, *Systematic Theology*, Vol. II, p. 52. Although somewhat ambivalent on this point, Tillich strongly hints that essence is never truly actualized in existence, that authentic existence is an impossibility, and estrangement a necessity.

17. *KD* II/2.

18. Karl Barth, *From Rousseau to Ritschl* (London: SCM Press, Ltd., 1959), pp. 12, 48–51, 338.

19. *KD* III/3, pp. 327–425.

20. Cf. John D. Godsey, *The Theology of Dietrich Bonhoeffer* (The Westminster Press, 1960), pp. 276–279.

21. Bonhoeffer's suggestion that the "religious a priori" is a dead option, that we live in a world "come of age" which has outgrown the need for religion, perhaps needs the corrective of Tillich's definition of religion as ultimate concern. If every man expresses ultimate concerns even in his mundane behavior, we can hardly agree that he has outgrown religion. Some who have followed Bonhoeffer's view of "religionless Christianity" and Tillich's view of the "latent church" have been tempted prematurely to cut their roots from the empirical church. Cf. Peter Berger, *The Noise of Solemn Assemblies* (Doubleday & Company, Inc., 1961), pp. 157 ff.

22. Reinhold Niebuhr has perhaps employed too strict a bifurcation between the "two spheres." Bonhoeffer has welded the two spheres into an indifferentiated whole, failing to distinguish God and history.

23. The same applies to Barth.

24. Cf. "Secular Authority: To What Extent It Should Be Obeyed" (1523), *Martin Luther*, Selections, pp. 363 ff. Cf. Bonhoeffer's *Ethics*, Parts I and II.

25. *KD* IV/2, pp. 612 ff. Cf. Dietrich Bonhoeffer, *The Cost of Discipleship* (The Macmillan Company, 1958), pp. 50 ff.

26. Subsequently we will offer certain criticisms of Bultmann's proposals that make us more inclined to regard his efforts as merely a new beginning rather than a finished plateau for a new phase of Protestant ethics. We would not wish prematurely to project the impression that we regard Bultmann's work as the only recourse for new directions in Protestant ethics (see Ch. V, C, for a prospectus). We have merely wished at this point to indicate how his endeavor dovetails with some persistent problems of current Protestant moral thought.

Chapter I. RADICAL OBEDIENCE

1. *Jesus* (Tübingen: J. C. B. Mohr, Paul Siebeck, 1951), pp. 67 f.; Eng. trans., *Jesus and the Word* (Charles Scribner's Sons, 1958), pp. 75 ff.

2. *Jesus Christ and Mythology* (Charles Scribner's Sons, 1958), pp. 11–21.

3. *Jesus*, pp. 27 ff., 33–36; *Das Urchristentum*, p. 75, (Zürich: Artemis-Verlag, 1949); Eng. trans. by R. H. Fuller, *Primitive Christianity in Its Contemporary Setting*, (Meridian Books, Inc., 1956).

4. *Jesus Christ and Mythology*, pp. 14 ff.

5. *Urchr.*, p. 97.

6. *Theologie des Neuen Testaments* (Tübingen: J. C. B. Mohr, 1954), pp. 1–3; Eng. trans. by Kendrick Grobel, *Theology of the New Testament* (Charles Scribner's Sons, 1951), I, pp. 3–5.

7. *Urchr.*, p. 99; cf. *Jesus*, pp. 33 ff.

8. *TNT*, pp. 10–12 (6–8).

9. *Ibid.*, pp. 19, 327 ff., 544–545.

10. "The Study of the Synoptic Gospels," in *Form Criticism* (Willet, Clark & Company, 1934), p. 24, trans. by F. C. Grant.

11. *Ibid.*, p. 72.

12. *Ibid.*, p. 73.

13. *TNT*, pp. 19 f.

14. *Ibid.*, p. 20.

15. *Ibid.*, p. 15.

16. *Jesus*, p. 64 (73).

17. *Ibid.*, pp. 67 ff.

18. *Urchr.*, p. 78 (72–73).

19. *Jesus*, p. 60 (66).

20. *Ibid.*, pp. 61–65 (66–71); *Urchr.*, p. 79 (72).

21. *TNT*, p. 10 (11); *Jesus*, p. 63 (68); *Urchr.*, pp. 72–74.

22. *Urchr.*, p. 75 (69).

23. *Jesus*, p. 62 (70–71); *Urchr.*, p. 77 (70 ff.); *TNT*, p. 10 (11).

24. *Urchr.*, p. 75 (70).

25. *Urchr.*, pp. 23 ff. (21 ff.).

26. *Jesus*, p. 77.

27. *Urchr.*, pp. 74–75.

28. "Das christliche Gebot der Nächstenliebe," *Glauben und Verstehen, Gesammelte Aufsätze*, I (Tübingen: J. C. B. Mohr, 1954), pp. 239–240.

29. *G.u.V.*, II, p. 156; Eng. trans. by James C. G. Greig,

Essays Philosophical and Theological (The Macmillan Company, 1955), p. 175.

30. *Jesus,* pp. 68 f.; *G.u.V.,* II, p. 157 (176).

31. *G.u.V.,* I, p. 239.

32. *Jesus,* pp. 76 ff. (88 ff.).

33. *Urchr.,* pp. 20 ff.

34. *Urchr.,* pp. 78 f. (71 ff.); *TNT,* p. 17 (19); *Jesus,* pp. 84 ff. (96). For a critique of this analogy, cf. Thomas C. Oden, "Is the Demand of God Ambiguous? An American-European Dialogue," *The Ecumenical Review,* XIII, No. 2 (Jan., 1961), pp. 166 ff.

35. *Jesus,* pp. 84 ff. (96 ff.).

36. *Urchr.,* pp. 96 ff. (86 ff.).

37. *Jesus,* pp. 71–72.

38. *Ibid.,* pp. 76–78.

39. *Dem Allgemeinen,* the universal or general, as contrasted with the particularity of the moment. *Jesus,* p. 77.

40. *Jesus,* pp. 78–79, 83.

41. *Ibid.,* p. 83.

42. Cf. Søren Kierkegaard, *Philosophical Fragments,* trans. by D. F. Swenson (Princeton University Press, 1936), pp. 1–10.

43. *Jesus,* p. 68 (77–78); cf. *Urchr.,* p. 86.

44. The *what* (*Was*) of an action is its concrete situational content, whereas the *that* (*Dass*) of an action is the formal fact that it is done.

45. *Jesus,* p. 82 (94).

46. *Ibid.,* p. 82.

47. It would indeed be nice if all moral situations were as simple and unambiguous as that portrayed by the parable of the good Samaritan, who was confronted by a man unjustly beaten, lying beside the road, desperately needing immediate help. The parable speaks of no conflicting obligations. The parable is far from analogous to most moral situations.

48. *TNT* (Grobel, trans.), p. 19.

49. Cf. Søren Kierkegaard, *Works of Love,* trans. by Lillian M. Swenson, (Princeton University Press, 1946), I. Bultmann's view of love is heavily dependent upon Kierkegaard.

50. *Urchr.,* pp. 78–80; *Jesus,* pp. 84 ff.; *TNT,* pp. 18 f.

51. Or the maxim, "Do unto others as you would have them do unto you."

52. "Das christliche Gebot der Nächstenliebe," *G.u.V.*, I, p. 239.

53. *Ibid.*, p. 239.

54. *Verborgenheit.* The meaning of love is concealed except in the act of love.

55. "Das christliche Gebot der Nächstenliebe," p. 240.

56. *TNT*, pp. 16 ff.; *Jesus*, pp. 97–99.

57. Cf. *Jesus*, pp. 98 ff.

58. *Jesus*, p. 100; cf. *Urchr.*, p. 86 (75 f.).

59. *Jesus*, pp. 100–101 (117 ff.).

60. *Jesus*, p. 101 (118).

61. *Ibid.*, p. 99 (115).

62. *Ibid.*, p. 102 (118); also "Das christliche Gebot der Nächstenliebe," *G.u.V.*, I, pp. 242 ff. The great difficulty with this idea is not that the neighbor continually meets me with his need, but that many different neighbors continually meet me with conflicting needs. Bultmann does not speak to this perplexity.

63. *Jesus*, p. 74 (84). Cf. "Die liberale Theologie und die jüngste theologische Bewegung," *G.u.V.*, I, pp. 15–18.

64. Jacques Maritain, *Existence and the Existent.* Trans. by L. Galantiere and G. Phelan (Pantheon Books, Inc., 1948).

65. "Die Eschatologie des Johannes-Evangeliums," *G.u.V.*, I, p. 139. Cf. Martin Heidegger, *Sein und Zeit*, I, pp. 41–130 (67–169), on the analysis of the concept *Dasein.*

66. *TNT*, p. 206 (209).

67. *Ibid.*, pp. 205–206.

68. "Die Eschatologie des Johannes-Evangeliums," *G.u.V.*, I, pp. 137–139. *Kosmos* refers to the created order in its fallenness, in the Fourth Gospel.

69. "Die Eschatologie des Johannes-Evangeliums," *G.u.V.*, I, pp. 139–141.

70. "Vom Schicksal," *Die christliche Welt*, XXXVI (1922), p. 609.

71. Bultmann spoke in a very early sermon of "the law of the eternally provisional" ("Unruhe und Ruhe," *Die christliche Welt* XXXVI [1922], pp. 569–570). Human life has no rest, it is constantly in slavery to the future. If it is not open to the future, it is not open to the present. Man artificially creates unrest when a moment of rest breaks in upon him because he

wishes to flee from himself. "The true rest which comes from God can only grow out of an unrest which is far more frightening than all the unrest of the world. But we shudder before this final unrest, and without admitting it to ourselves flee from it into the unrest of the world."

72. "The Understanding of Man and the World in the N.T. and in the Greek World," *Essays Philosophical and Theological*, pp. 78 f.

73. Cf. *supra*, pp. 41 ff.

74. "The Crisis in Belief," *Essays*, p. 8.

75. *Ibid.*, p. 7.

76. *Ibid.*, p. 9.

77. Despite this, however, Bultmann argues that Greek ethics was preconsciously based upon an understanding of action as taking place in the relation between an I and a Thou, however much the existentiality of this relation became lost in rational analysis, since the original meanings of the virtues of wisdom, courage, temperance, and justice were not only that one ought to embody within himself the qualities of wisdom, courage, temperance, or justice, but that one ought to *act wisely*, courageously, temperately, and justly. "Das christliche Gebot der Nächstenliebe" *G.u.V.*, I, pp. 232–233.

78. *Ibid.*, p. 233; *Jesus*, pp. 75, 82–86 (91–95).

CHAPTER II. EXISTENTIAL ANALYSIS OF HUMAN OBLIGATION

1. Schubert M. Ogden, "Bultmann's Project of Demythologization and the Problem of Theology and Philosophy," in *The Journal of Religion*, XXXVII, No. 3 (July, 1957), pp. 156–173.

2. *Ibid.*, p. 166. "For, while he does not explicitly deny that unqualified demythologization is possible, he does explicitly deny that theology and philosophy are . . . identical." Ogden argues that "the implication of his explicit affirmation of the possibility of demythologization is that theology and philosophy are finally indistinguishable."

3. *Ibid.*, p. 168. "The traditional notion of a unique salvation event in history which is unamenable to demythologization and is therefore capable of establishing a distinction between

theology and philosophy simply cannot be maintained. . . . If theology of today is to face responsibly the situation in which it actually finds itself and, at the same time, is to avoid intolerable inconsistencies, it has no other choice than frankly to acknowledge its ultimate identity with the 'right philosophy,' i.e., with the object of man's disciplined efforts to explicate the understanding of existence that is given with his existence itself." (Pp. 170–171).

4. "The New Testament and Mythology," *Kerygma and Myth*. Cf. also "Jesus Christ and Mythology" for an explication on this distinction.

5. Cf. Thomas C. Oden, "The Idea of Obedience in Contemporary Protestant Ethics," Ch. 1 (Yale dissertation, 1960), for an elaboration of this distinction.

6. Gerhardt Kuhlmann, "Zum theologischen Problem der Existenz: Fragen an Rudolf Bultmann," *Zeitschrift für Theologie und Kirche*, Neue Folge, X (1929), pp. 28–57.

7. "Die Geschichtlichkeit des Daseins und der Glaube: Antwort an Gerhardt Kuhlmann," in *Zeitschrift für Theologie und Kirche*, XI (1930), pp. 339–364, trans. by Schubert M. Ogden, *Existence and Faith*, pp. 92–110.

8. *Daseinsanalyse* means analysis of human existence, or existential analysis of man, as it has been used by Heidegger and Bultmann. *Dasein* might be rendered variously as "human existence," "man," "the existing individual," or "personal existence."

9. "The Historicity of Man and Faith," *E & F*, p. 93.

10. *Ibid.*, pp. 94 ff.

11. *Ibid.*, pp. 95 ff.

12. *TNT*, p. 191. Cf. pp. 125–126. Cf. Heidegger, *Being and Time*.

13. *Ibid.*, pp. 197 ff. Cf. Ogden, "Bultmann's Project of Demythologization and the Problem of Theology and Philosophy," *loc. cit.*, p. 167.

14. *Ibid.*, pp. 208 f.

15. "The Historicity of Man and Faith," *E & F*, pp. 94–97.

16. John Macquarrie, *An Existentialist Theology* (London: SCM Press, Ltd., 1955), p. 34.

17. "The Historicity of Man and Faith," *E & F*, *passim*.

18. Ogden, "Bultmann's Project of Demythologization and

the Problem of Theology and Philosophy," *loc. cit.*, pp. 168–169.

19. *TNT*, p. 192.

20. *Ibid.*, p. 199.

21. *Ibid.*, p. 191.

22. *Ibid.*, p. 197.

23. His being is always "out of something" (*im Aus-sein auf etwas*). He gains "life" from some goal. *Ibid.*, p. 205.

24. *TNT*, p. 206.

25. *Ibid.*, p. 206: "Das Ziel der Richtung ist in der ontologischen Struktur des Gerichtetseins noch nicht festgelegt . . ."

26. *Ibid.*, pp. 205–207.

27. *Ibid.*, pp. 222 ff.

28. *TNT*, pp. 216 ff.

29. *Ibid.*, p. 222.

30. *Ibid.*, p. 223.

31. *Ibid.*, p. 235 (239).

32. "Römer 7 und die Anthropologie des Paulus," in *Imago Dei* (Festschrift für G. Krüger), pp. 53–62 (Giessen: Alfred Töpelmann, 1932); trans. by Schubert M. Ogden, *E & F*, pp. 147 ff.

33. *TNT*, pp. 208 ff. (211 ff.).

34. *Ibid.*, p. 209.

35. *Urchr.*, p. 202.

36. *Ibid.*, p. 202. ". . . der faktische Wille gar nicht wollen kann, was er eigentlich will."

37. Rom. 7:15, 19; cf. "Römer 7 und die Anthropologie des Paulus," *loc. cit.*, pp. 57 ff. (151 ff.).

38. "Das christliche Gebot der Nächstenliebe," *G.u.V.*, I, pp. 233–234.

39. *Ibid.*, pp. 233 ff.

40. *Jesus*, p. 60 (66); cf. *supra*, sections 2 and 3.

41. *Essays*.

42. *E & F*.

43. *G.u.V.*, I.

44. Thomas C. Oden, "The Idea of Obedience in Contemporary Protestant Ethics," Part II, Ch. 2.

45. *Ibid.*, Ch. 1.

46. *Jesus Christ and Mythology* (Charles Scribner's Sons, 1958), p. 52.

47. *Ibid.*, p. 52 (italics mine).

48. "The Problem of Hermeneutics," *Essays*, p. 257.

49. "The Concept of Revelation in the New Testament," *E & F.*, pp. 58–91. Revelation in this sense may be either the communication of knowledge, or an event that places the self in a new situation. All religions speak of revelation in one or the other way.

50. *Ibid.*, pp. 60 ff.

51. *Ibid.*, pp. 64 ff.

52. *Ibid.*, Part III, pp. 71 ff.

53. "The Crisis in Belief," *Essays*, p. 7.

54. *Ibid.*, p. 3.

55. *Ibid.*, p. 4.

56. The enigma of God is a persistent theme in Bultmann's theology, for as early as 1917 he was speaking of a mysterious God, full of contradictions and riddles. Yet enigma and mystery lose their meaning when they do not lead us to want and thirst for his own self-disclosure. "Concerning the Hidden and the Revealed God," in *E & F*, pp. 23 ff.

57. "The Crisis in Belief," *Essays*, pp. 5–6. (H. Richard Niebuhr's article, "The Nature and Existence of God," *motive* magazine [Dec., 1943], Part II, follows a similar pattern.)

58. *Ibid.*, p. 5.

59. "Die Frage der natürlichen Offenbarung," *G.u.V.*, II, originally in *Offenbarung und Heilsgeschehen* (Tübingen: J. C. B. Mohr, 1941), pp. 3–26.

60. *Ibid.*, pp. 81–82 (95–96).

61. *Ibid.*, p. 82.

62. "The Crisis in Belief," *Essays*, pp. 2 ff. Cf. "The Question of Natural Revelation," and "Das Problem der 'Natürlichen Theologie.'" This would lead one to assume that Bultmann accepts Barth's critique of natural theology, except for his notion of the knowability of God as limiter.

63. *Jesus Christ and Mythology*, p. 52; cf. *supra*, section 2.

64. This ambiguity is most clearly seen with a careful reading of the essay on "The Question of Natural Revelation"; cf. also "The Crisis in Belief."

65. "The Question of Natural Revelation," pp. 95 ff.

66. *Ibid.*, p. 95.

67. *Ibid.*, p. 96.

68. *Ibid.*, p. 96.

69. *Ibid.*, p. 94.

70. *Ibid.*, pp. 96–97. Cf. "Welchen Sinn hat es, von Gott zu reden?", *G.u.V.*, I, pp. 26–29.

71. John Macquarrie, *The Scope of Demythology* (Harper & Row, Publishers, Inc., 1960).

72. *TNT*, p. 212 (I, 216).

73. *Ibid.*, pp. 208 ff. (211 ff.).

74. *Ibid.*, pp. 213–214.

75. *Ibid.*, p. 214.

76. *Urchr.*, pp. 201–202 (181).

77. Faith and obedience, *TNT*, p. 216.

78. I Cor. 4:3.

79. *TNT*, p. 214 (218).

80. *Ibid.*, p. 215 (italics mine).

81. *Transzendente Instanz, TNT*, p. 216.

82. *TNT*, p. 215: *"Und wie hier die syneidēsis, ursprünglich das Wissen des Menschen, objektiviert ist und metonymisch für die Instanz eingetreten ist, um die das Wissen die syneidēsis weiss, so wird Rm 9, 1; 2 Kr 1, 12 die syneidēsis zu einer jenseits des Menschen stehenden Instanz objektiviert ('personifiziert'), worin eben zur Erscheinung kommt, dass die Bindung an die transzendente Instanz das Wesentliche bei die syneidēsis ist."*

83. *Urchr.*, pp. 115–132 (103 ff.); "Polis und Hades in der Antigone des Sophokles," "Das Verständnis von Welt und Mensch im Neuen Testament und im Griechentum," *G.u.V.*, II, pp. 20 ff., 59 ff. (22 ff., 67 ff.).

84. *G.u.V.*, II, p. 59.

85. *Ibid.*, p. 69; *Urchr.*, p. 122 (109).

86. *Urchr.*, p. 118 (105).

87. *G.u.V.*, II, p. 59 (67).

88. *Ibid.*, p. 60 (68).

89. *Ibid.*, p. 61 (69).

90. *Ibid.*, p. 61 (69).

91. *G.u.V.*, II, pp. 20 ff., 51, 60, 63, 223–224 (22 ff., 58, 68, 70, 248).

92. *Ibid.*, pp. 20–21 (22–23).

93. *Ibid.*, p. 23 (26).

94. *Ibid.*, p. 25 (28).

95. *Ibid.*, pp. 23–26. Cf. *Urchr.*, p. 124 (110).
96. *Urchr.*, pp. 125–126 (112).
97. *G.u.V.*, II, p. 62 (70).
98. *Ibid.*, p. 63 (71).
99. *Ibid.*, p. 62 (70).
100. *Ibid.*, pp. 61 ff.; *Urchr.*, pp. 129 ff. (115 ff.).
101. *Urchr.*, p. 129 (115).
102. *Urchr.*, p. 125 (112).
103. *G.u.V.*, II, pp. 65 ff. (74).
104. *Urchr.*, p. 161 (143).
105. *Ibid.*, pp. 157 ff. (139 ff.).
106. *Ibid.*, p. 161 (143).
107. *Ibid.*, p. 161.
108. *Ibid.*, p. 161, quoted from Hans Jonas, *Augustin und das paulinische Freiheitsproblem* (1930), p. 12.
109. *G.u.V.*, II, p. 63 (72).
110. *Urchr.*, pp. 151 ff. (136 ff.).
111. *G.u.V.*, II, p. 65 (74); *Urchr.*, p. 152 (135 ff.).
112. *Urchr.*, p. 154 (138).
113. *Urchr.*, p. 155.
114. *G.u.V.*, II, pp. 63 ff. (67 ff.); *Urchr.*, p. 161 (143).

CHAPTER III. THE CHRISTIAN PROCLAMATION
AS THE TRANSFORMATION OF ETHICS

1. "Neues Testament und Mythologie," *Kerygma und Mythos* I, ed. by H. W. Bartsch, 2d ed. (Hamburg: Herbert Reich-Evangelischer Verlag, 1951), p. 40. This translation by S. M. Ogden (*op. cit.*), p. 168. *Kerygma and Myth*, trans. by R. H. Fuller (London: S.P.C.K. 1957), p. 33.

2. *Ibid.*, p. 32 (23).

3. *Ibid.*, p. 32 (24); or Jaspers' philosophy might appear to be a transposition of Kierkegaard's interpretation of Christian existence. The real problem disturbing Bultmann is not that of the theologian borrowing categories from philosophy, but that the philosophers seem to be saying much the same thing about human existence as the New Testament, and saying it quite independently.

4. *Ibid.*, p. 33 (25).
5. *Ibid.*, p. 34 (26).
6. *Ibid.*, p. 34 (27).

7. *Ibid.,* pp. 32–35; cf. "Die Geschichtlichkeit des Daseins und der Glaube," *loc. cit.,* pp. 340 ff. (95 ff.).

8. *Ibid.,* p. 34 (27).

9. *KM,* I, p. 35 (28).

10. "Die Geschichtlichkeit des Daseins und der Glaube," *loc. cit.,* p. 345.

11. *KM,* I, p. 35 (28). Bultmann stands squarely with Luther and Calvin in this connection. The point at issue is "how we understand the fall." The philosophical tradition assumes that all man needs is to be shown his plight to be able to escape from it. It fails to see that man's fallenness extends to man's inmost self, whereas the New Testament regards man's fallenness as total. Cf. Calvin's *Institutes,* I. iv.

12. *KM,* I, p. 36 (29).

13. *Ibid.,* pp. 36 f. (30).

14. *Ibid.,* p. 38 (30).

15. *Eigenmächtigkeit,* a synonym for "disobedience" for Bultmann.

16. *KM,* I, p. 38 (30–31).

17. *Ibid.,* p. 38 (31); cf. *TNT,* pp. 284 ff.

18. *KM,* I, p. 38 (31).

19. II Cor. 5:17; John 3:3 ff.

20. *TNT,* pp. 296 ff. (321 ff.). *KM,* I, pp. 38 f. (31–32).

21. *KM,* I, pp. 39–40 (32–33).

22. *Essays,* pp. 10, 109–113.

23. *Gott als eines Gegenüber, ibid.,* pp. 11–12.

24. *Ibid.,* p. 11.

25. *Ibid.,* p. 12.

26. "Zum Problem der Entmythologisierung," *KM,* II, ed. by H. W. Bartsch (Hamburg: Herbert Reich-Evangelischer Verlag, 1952), p. 184.

27. *KM,* II, p. 184, "To know Christ is to know his benefits."

28. *Ibid.,* p. 195.

29. *Ibid.,* pp. 196–197. Cf. Erich Frank, *Philosophical Understanding and Religious Truth* (Oxford University Press, 1945), pp. 44, 161–164.

30. *KM,* II, p. 197.

31. *Ibid.,* p. 197. Radical obedience in fact is defined as responding to the demand of the moment as if it were the demand of God.

32. "Das Problem der Hermeneutik," *G.u.V.*, II, p. 233 (260); *dem Verschiedenen.*

33. To be historical (*geschichtlich*) means for Bultmann to exist in encounter, in meeting with others. Thus the love of another encounters me as what it is only as event. It cannot be perceived by objectifying vision. Seen from "the outside," it is not truly love.

34. *KM*, II, p. 201.

35. Emil Brunner, *The Christian Doctrine of Creation and Redemption, Dogmatics*, II, trans. by Olive Wyon (The Westminster Press, 1952), pp. 268 ff., makes this criticism. Cf. W. G. Kümmel, *Mythische Rede und Heilsgeschehen im Neuen Testament* (Lund: Coniectanea Neotestamentica, 1947).

36. *KM*, II, p. 203.

37. *Ibid.*, p. 204.

38. *Ibid.*, p. 205. Thus Bultmann does not share the concern of Amos Wilder and others in protecting the *Historie* of Jesus.

39. *Ibid.*, p. 206.

40. *Ibid.*, p. 206. The church as the eschatological community of the called, says Bultmann, is "only paradoxically identical with the sociological phenomenon or institutional structure."

41. *G.u.V.*, II, p. 86 (98).

42. *Ibid.*, pp. 90 ff. (102 ff.).

43. *Vorverständnis.*

44. *Ibid.*, p. 89 (102). "God is not the moral law, but the Holy One" (*der Heilige*). That which is known in reason's moral law (Kant) is not God, but just oneself. The man who sees himself under the demand of the *Heilige* disclosed in the Christ event knows himself as a sinner rather than a "knower" of God's demand.

45. *G.u.V.*, II, pp. 93 (106).

46. *Ibid.*, pp. 91 ff. (104 ff.).

47. *Ibid.*, pp. 93–94 (107–108).

48. *G.u.V.*, II, pp. 95 ff. (109).

49. *G.u.V.*, I, from *Theologische Blätter*, III, 1924; p. 18.

50. *Ibid.*, pp. 18 ff. Cf. Karl Barth, *The Epistle to the Romans* (London: Oxford University Press, 1933), pp. 42 ff.

51. *Ibid.*, p. 20.

52. *TNT*, p. 310 (314).
53. *Jesus Christ and Mythology*, p. 41.
54. *Urchr.*, p. 226 (202).
55. *Jesus Christ and Mythology*, p. 40.
56. *TNT*, p. 310 (314); "Glaubensakt als Gehorsamsakt."
57. *Ibid.*, p. 311 (315).
58. *Ibid.*, pp. 238 ff. (240 ff.); "Glaube als Gehorsam."
59. *TNT*, p. 312 (317); "faith equals obedience."
60. *Ibid.*, p. 313 (317–318).
61. *Ibid.*, p. 315; "anhaftende Qualität."
62. *TNT*, p. 315 (319). "... so ist ihre Gegenwärtigkeit kein zeitlicher und als solcher vergänglicher Zustand."
63. *Ibid.*, p. 316 (319).
64. *Ibid.*, p. 317 (320).
65. Der Glaube als Wagnis," *Die Christliche Welt*, xlii, 42 (1928), p. 1009 (*E & F*, pp. 55 ff.).
66. *Ibid.*, p. 1010 (57).
67. *TNT*, p. 318; "das Überwundene."
68. *Ibid.*, p. 318.
69. *Ibid.*, p. 319.
70. *Ibid.*, pp. 319 ff.
71. *Ibid.*, p. 320.
72. *Ibid.*, pp. 271–273.
73. *TNT*, p. 323.
74. *Ibid.*, p. 313.
75. *Ibid.*, pp. 313–314.
76. *TNT*, p. 314.
77. *Ibid.*, p. 313.
78. "Bestimmtheit des Konkreten Lebens," *ibid.*, p. 324.
79. "Ins Einzelne," such as speech, friendly reception, greetings, according to Paul.
80. *TNT*, pp. 153–157.
81. *Ibid.*, pp. 158 ff.
82. *TNT*, pp. 155 ff.

CHAPTER IV. INDICATIVE AND IMPERATIVE

1. *TNT*, p. 428.
2. *Ibid.*, pp. 329 ff.
3. *Ibid.*, p. 329.

4. Goethe, Hegel, *et al.*: "Become who you are!"

5. *TNT*, pp. 421 ff., 266 ff., 329 f.

6. *Ibid.*, p. 428; "aus dem Empfang der Liebe entspringt die Verpflichtung zum Lieben."

7. John 15:10.

8. John 15:10; cf. *TNT*, p. 428.

9. Phil. 3:12–14; cf. *TNT*, p. 100.

10. Gal. 5:1–6.

11. Cf. Gordon Kaufman's concept of "time binding," *The Context of Decision* (Abingdon Press, 1961), pp. 72–80.

12. Barth in contrast would speak of the saving deed of God as an ontological actuality, never as mere "possibility."

13. "What fundamentally has happened," Bultmann declares, "must be realized in practice," *TNT*, p. 100 (*Was grundsätzlich geschehen ist, gilt es praktisch zu realisieren*).

14. *Ibid.*, pp. 100–103.

15. *Ibid.*, p. 102. Cf. *Jesus Christ and Mythology*, pp. 76–77.

16. *Ibid.*, p. 161 (162–163).

17. *Ibid.*, sections 51–61.

18. *Ibid.*, pp. 544–545.

19. *TNT*, p. 552.

20. I Clem. 30:1; *TNT*, p. 529.

21. *Ibid.*, pp. 516 ff.

22. *Ibid.*, section 58, "Christology and Soteriology."

23. Cf. *supra*, Ch. II, D, 1 and 2.

24. Also found in Barth's ethics; *Church Dogmatics* II/2, III/4.

25. *TNT*, p. 327.

26. *Ibid.*, p. 328.

27. *Jesus Christ and Mythology*, p. 77.

28. *TNT*, p. 328.

29. *Ibid.*, pp. 327 f.

30. *Jesus Christ and Mythology*, pp. 76 ff.

31. For it is not the business of philosophy to proclaim to man that he is loved in the midst of his situation with an infinite forgiving love that would free him from self-assertiveness and for authentic selfhood.

32. *Jesus Christ and Mythology*, p. 78.

33. *History and Eschatology*, pp. 14 ff.

34. *Jesus Christ and Mythology*, p. 76.

35. *TNT*, p. 332.
36. *Jesus*, p. 73.
37. Cf. *supra*, Ch. I.
38. *Jesus*, p. 74.
39. *TNT*, p. 256.
40. *Ibid.*, p. 255.
41. *G.u.V.*, II, p. 32.
42. *G.u.V.*, II, p. 36n.
43. *Supra*, Ch. II, C, 3; Ch. III, A, 1.
44. *G.u.V.*, II, pp. 35–36, 44–45; *E & F*, "Romans 7 and the Anthropology of Paul," p. 147–157.
45. Bultmann notes that Paul's utterances about his past do not indicate that he suffered from an oppressive consciousness of sin. Perhaps this is why the concept of repentance plays so little part in Paul's theology. He thought of himself as "blameless" in fulfilling the law (Phil. 3:4 ff.) and a zealot for the traditions of his fathers (Gal. 1:13 ff.). Bultmann disagrees with the view that Rom., ch. 7, describes the tension within the Christian between the old and new man. Rather, it describes the old man's situation, which can be seen only from the perspective of the new man.
46. "Der eigentliche Wille," *TNT*, p. 255.
47. *G.u.V.*, II, p. 41.
48. *Ibid.*, p. 47.
49. *Ibid.*, p. 41.
50. "Righteousness" in the Jewish sense, Bultmann explains, is not a quality that adheres to man, but a verdict understood only in relation to God. It means the affirmation accorded man by the pronouncement of the judge (God). When the judge's verdict establishes the righteousness of the accused, he is given the "right" of it, i.e., the acknowledgment of his innocence, the vindication of his challenged honor. Jewish righteousness, warns Bultmann, must not be confused with Plato's moral perfection, or Goethe's striving for self-perfection.
51. *G.u.V.*, II, pp. 38–40, 46.
52. *Ibid.*, pp. 41–42.
53. *Ibid.*, p. 48.
54. *TNT*, pp. 336–338; cf. *G.u.V.*, II, p. 53.
55. I Cor. 6:12; 10:23.
56. *TNT*, pp. 262, 263, 267.

57. *Supra,* Ch. I, C.
58. *TNT,* p. 340.
59. "Das christliche Gebot der Nächstenliebe," *G.u.V.,* I, p. 241; cf. *KM,* I, pp. 38 ff. (30 ff.).
60. *G.u.V.,* II, p. 12 (13).
61. *G.u.V.,* I, p. 242; cf. *KM,* I, p. 39 (31).
62. *Ibid.,* pp. 243, 244.
63. *G.u.V.,* I, p. 244.
64. *G.u.V.,* II, p. 10 (11).
65. *Ibid.,* pp. 10–12 (11–13); cf. *Zeitschrift für Missionskunde und Religionswissenschaft,* "Der Sinn des christlichen Schöpfungsglaubens," LI (1936), p. 11.
66. *G.u.V.,* I, p. 230.
67. *Ibid.,* p. 230; cf. *Jesus,* pp. 95 ff.
68. *G.u.V.,* I, p. 321.
69. "Die Eschatologie des Johannes-Evangeliums," *G.u.V.,* I, pp. 149–150.
70. *G.u.V.,* I, p. 235.
71. *Ibid.,* p. 240.
72. *Ibid.,* pp. 235–236.
73. *Ibid.,* p. 240.
74. *Ibid.,* p. 237 ("Die Liebe ist überhaupt keine Eigenschaft, kein Was am Menschen, sondern ein Wie seines Miteinanderseins").
75. *Ibid.,* p. 238.
76. *Ibid.,* p. 242.
77. *Supra,* Ch. IV, D, 1.
78. *TNT,* pp. 339 ff.
79. *Ibid.,* p. 341.
80. I Cor. 9:20; *TNT,* p. 340.
81. *G.u.V.,* I, pp. 234–235.
82. The Kantian theme that one loves solely because one *ought* to love, rather than because he is inclined to, is present in Bultmann.
83. Søren Kierkegaard, *Works of Love,* trans. by L. M. Swenson (Princeton University Press, 1946).
84. *G.u.V.,* II, p. 70 (70).
85. Søren Kierkegaard, *Concluding Unscientific Postscript,* trans. by D. F. Swenson (Princeton University Press, 1944), pp. 107 ff.

86. *G.u.V.*, II, p. 70 (79).

87. Cf. *G.u.V.*, I, pp. 234–235.

88. *Zeitschrift für Missionskunde und Religionswissenschaft*, LI, pp. 16–18.

89. *TNT*, II, *passim; G.u.V.*, I, pp. 134 ff., 294 ff., II, pp. 1 ff., 59 ff., 79 ff.

90. Friedrich Gogarten, *Demythologizing and History* (Charles Scribner's Sons, 1955), *passim;* Martin Heidegger, *Sein und Zeit* (Tübingen: Neomarius Verlag, 1949).

91. "Die Geschichtlichkeit des Daseins und der Glaube," *loc. cit.*, p. 354 (*E & F*, pp. 92 ff.).

92. *Ibid.*, p. 356.

93. *Ibid.*, pp. 356–358.

94. *Ibid.*, p. 359.

95. *Ibid.*, pp. 357 ff.

96. *Ibid.*, pp. 356–358.

97. *Ibid.*, pp. 360 ff.

98. *Ibid.*, p. 362.

CHAPTER V. CONCLUDING CRITIQUE

1. This anomaly in ethics parallels Heidegger's "overcoming" of metaphysics.

2. *Jesus Christ and Mythology*, p. 52.

3. Cf. H. Richard Niebuhr, *Christ and Culture* (Harper & Row, Publishers, Inc., 1951), pp. 11–29; *Radical Monotheism and Western Culture* (Harper & Row, Publishers, Inc., 1960), pp. 100–127.

4. *Supra,* Ch. I, A; II, B; IV, D.

5. *Supra,* Ch. I, A; B.

6. *Supra,* Ch. II, A; B; C.

7. Cf. esp. Reinhold Niebuhr. Also Simone de Beauvoir, *The Ethics of Ambiguity,* tr. by Bernard Frechtman (Citadel Press, 1962).

8. Cf. Erich Fromm, *Man for Himself* (Holt, Rinehart and Winston, 1947), pp. 119 ff.

9. A fresh approach to this issue is taken in Gordon Kaufman's *The Context of Decision*, pp. 89–116.

10. Cf. Albert Outler, *The Christian Tradition and the*

Unity We Seek (Oxford University Press, 1957), pp. 105 ff.

11. *Ein Wort Lutherischer Theologie,* ed. E. Kinder (Evangelischer Presseverband für Bayern, 1952).

12. Karl Jaspers and Rudolf Bultmann, *Myth and Christianity* (The Noonday Press, 1958), pp. 3–57.

13. E.g., Barth's concept of the obedience of Jesus Christ in our place, *KD* IV/1, section 59.

14. Friedrich Schleiermacher, *The Christian Faith* (Edinburgh: T. & T. Clark, 1928), pp. 16 ff.

15. Dietrich Bonhoeffer, *Ethics* (London: SCM Press, Ltd., 1955), pp. 271 ff., has offered a fresh approach to the first use of the law.

16. *Supra,* pp. 102 ff.

17. *Love and Justice* (The Westminster Press, 1957), p. 60. *Essays in Applied Christianity,* ed. by E. B. Robertson (Living Age Books, 1959), pp. 92, 100 ff., 175.

18. John Bennett, *Christian Social Action* (London: Lutterworth Press, 1954), pp. 64 ff. Alfred de Quervain, *Ethik,* 4 Bde (Zürich, 1945–1956); cf. also *Die theologischen Voraussetzungen der Politik,* 1931.

19. E. L. Long, *Conscience and Compromise* (The Westminster Press, 1954), pp. 141 ff., notes some of these dangers.

20. Paul Ramsey, *Basic Christian Ethics,* pp. 76 ff., 83 ff., and *Nine Modern Moralists, passim,* probes the alternative of a Protestant conception of natural law with wisdom and insight.

21. Paul Tillich, *Theology of Culture,* ed. by Robert C. Kimball (Oxford University Press, 1959), pp. 68–69.

22. Nicolai Hartmann, *Ethics,* Vol. Two: *Moral Values* (London: George Allen & Unwin, Ltd., 1931).

23. Charles Hartshorne, *Reality as Social Process* (Beacon Press, Inc., 1953).

24. H. Richard Niebuhr, *Radical Monotheism and Western Culture,* pp. 100 ff.

25. Ludwig Binswanger, *Grundformen und Erkenntnis Menschlichen Daseins* (Zürich: Niehans, 1953). Cf. "Existential Analysis and Psychotherapy," in Frieda Fromm-Reichmann and J. Moreno's *Progress in Psychotherapy* (Grune & Stratton, Inc., 1956), pp. 144 ff.

26. Harry Stack Sullivan, *Conceptions of Modern Psychiatry* (Washington, D.C.; William A. White Psychiatric Foundation, 1947); cf. "The Meaning of Anxiety in Psychiatry and in Life," *Psychiatry*, 11:1–13.

27. Carl Rogers, *Client-Centered Therapy* (Houghton Mifflin Company, 1951).

28. Karen Horney, *Neurosis and Human Growth* (W. W. Norton & Company, Inc., 1950).

29. Carl Rogers, *On Becoming a Person* (Houghton Mifflin Company, 1961), pp. 183–198.

30. Heinrich Schlier, "*Kerygma* und *Sophia*, zur neutestamentlichen Grundlegung des Dogmas," *Evangelische Theologie*, 1950–1951, pp. 481 ff.

31. Hans Küng, *The Council and Reunion* (London and New York: Sheed & Ward, 1961).

32. Karl Rahner, *Theological Investigations* (Helicon Press, 1960), Vol. I.

33. For a full account of this significant development see *Laici in Ecclesia*, published by the Department on the Laity, World Council of Churches, Geneva, 1961.

34. Robert Lowry Calhoun, *God and the Common Life* (The Shoe String Press, 1935).

RESPONSE

1. The original dissertation manuscript included a critical analysis of Barth's doctrine of obedience.

2. *KD* II/2, pp. 603 f. (543 f.).

3. *KD* II/2, p. 601.

SELECTED BIBLIOGRAPHY

A FULL bibliography of Bultmann's writings to 1954 may be found in "Veröffentlichungen von Rudolf Bultmann," *Theologische Rundschau*, XXII (1954), pp. 3–20. A further list of Bultmann's writings from 1954 to 1959 as well as a bibliography of works by him available in English and a representative selection of works dealing with his theology, may be found in *Existence and Faith*, ed. by Schubert M. Ogden (Meridian Books, Inc., 1960), pp. 317–320. The following list includes selected writings by Bultmann which pertain to ethical analysis.

Der Stil der Paulinischen Predigt und die kynisch-stoische Diatribe. Doctoral thesis, Göttingen, 1910.

"Das religiöse Moment in der ethischen Unterweisung der Epiktet und das Neue Testament," *Zeitschrift für die neutestamentliche Wissenschaft*, XIII, (1912), pp. 97–110.

"Religion und Kultur," *Die Christliche Welt*, XXXIV (1920), pp. 417–421; 435–439; 450–453.

"Ethische und mystische Religion im Urchristentum," *Die Christliche Welt*, XXXIV, (1920), pp. 725–731; 738–743.

"Das Problem der Ethik bei Paulus," *Zeitschrift für die neutestamentliche Wissenschaft*, XXIII (1924), pp. 123–140.

"Der christliche Sinn von Glaube, Liebe, Hoffnung," *Zeitschrift für den evangelische Religionsunterricht*, XXXVI, pp. 170–172.

Jesus. 2d ed. Berlin: Deutsche Bibliothek, 1929. English translation by L. P. Smith and Erminie Huntress: *Jesus and the Word.* Charles Scribner's Sons, 1934.

"Aimer son prochain, commandement de Dieu," *Revue d'histoire et de philosophie religieuses*, X (1930), pp. 222–

241. Reprinted in German as pp. 229–244 of *Glauben und Verstehen, I.* English translation by R. G. Smith: "To Love Your Neighbor," *The Scottish Periodical,* I, 1 (Summer, 1947), pp. 42–56.

Glauben und Verstehen, I, Gesammelte Aufsätze. Tübingen: J. C. B. Mohr, 1933.

"Gott ruft uns" (Sermon), *Neuwerk,* XIV (1933), pp. 70–81.

"Die Bergpredigt Jesu und das Recht des Staates," *Forschungen und Fortschritte,* XII (1936), pp. 101 f., E & F, pp. 202–205.

Das Evangelium des Johannes. Göttingen: Vandenhoeck und Ruprecht, 1941.

"Neues Testament und Mythologie: Das Problem der Entmythologisierung der neutestamentlichen Verkündigung," *Offenbarung und Heilsgeschehen: Beiträge zur Evangelische Theologie,* VII (1941), pp. 27–69. Reprinted as pp. 15–53 of *Kerygma und Mythos* I. Ed. by H. W. Bartsch. Hamburg: Herbert Reich-Evangelischer Verlag, 1948. English translation by R. H. Fuller: "New Testament and Mythology," *Kerygma and Myth.* London: S.P.C.K., 1953, pp. 1–44.

Review of J. Schmidt, *Ethos, Theologische Literaturzeitung* LXVIII (1943), pp. 205–206.

Das Urchristentum im Rahmen der antiken Religionen. Zürich: Artemis Verlag, 1949. English translation by R. H. Fuller; *Primitive Christianity in its Contemporary Setting.* London: Thames and Hudson, 1956; also New York: Meridian Books, Inc., 1956.

Glauben und Verstehen, II. Tübingen: J. C. B. Mohr, 1952, English translation by J. C. G. Greig: *Essays, Philosophical and Theological.* London: SCM Press, Ltd., 1955.

Theologie des Neuen Testaments, I, II, III. Tübingen: J. C. B. Mohr, 1948–1953. English translation by Kendrick Grobel: *Theology of the New Testament I, II.* Charles Scribner's Sons, 1951–1955.

Marburger Predigten. Tübingen: J. C. B. Mohr, 1956. English translation by Harold Knight, *This World and the Beyond.* Charles Scribner's Sons, 1960.

History and Eschatology. Edinburgh: Edinburgh University Press, 1957. The Gifford Lectures. American edition title: *The Presence of Eternity.* Harper & Row, Publishers, Inc., 1957.

Jesus Christ and Mythology. Charles Scribner's Sons, 1958. The Shaffer Lectures.

Myth and Christianity: An Inquiry Into the Possibility of Religion Without Myth (with Karl Jaspers). The Noonday Press, 1958.

"Theology for Freedom and Responsibility," *The Christian Century,* LXXV (1958), pp. 967–969.

"Preaching: Genuine and Secularized," *Religion and Culture: Essays in Honor of Paul Tillich,* ed. W. Leibrecht, Harper & Row, Publishers, Inc., 1959, pp. 236–242.

INDEX